FUNDAMENTALS OF MANTRACKING:

THE STEP-BY-STEP METHOD

FUNDAMENTALS OF MANTRACKING:
THE STEP-BY-STEP METHOD

AN ESSENTIAL PRIMER FOR SEARCH AND RESCUE TRACKERS

Third Edition

**Albert "Ab" Taylor
and
Donald C. Cooper**

SKYHORSE PUBLISHING

Copyright © 1990, 1992, 2014 Donald C. Cooper

Publication history:
First Printing, First Edition, April 1990
Second Printing, First Edition, December 1990
First Printing, Second Edition, January 1992
Second Printing, Second Edition, June 1993

This Third Edition is the first edition published by Skyhorse Publishing.

Skyhorse Publishing books may be purchased in bulk at special discounts for sales promotion, corporate gifts, fund-raising, or educational purposes. Special editions can also be created to specifications. For details, contact the Special Sales Department, Skyhorse Publishing, 307 West 36th Street, 11th Floor, New York, NY 10018 or info@skyhorsepublishing.com.

Skyhorse® and Skyhorse Publishing® are registered trademarks of Skyhorse Publishing, Inc.®, a Delaware corporation.

Visit our website at www.skyhorsepublishing.com.

10 9 8 7 6 5

Library of Congress Cataloging-in-Publication Data is available on file.

Cover design by David Sankey
Cover photo credit by Thinkstock

Print ISBN: 978-1-62914-762-8
Ebook ISBN: 978-1-62914-961-5

THE DEDICATION:

In loving memory of
Albert Snow Taylor, 1924 – 2013. He inspired
generations with unparalleled dedication to his
craft, his family, and the vulnerable,
and
Minnifred Taylor Lewis
who lived for, and loved, children.

A hundred years from now it will not matter what my bank
account was, the sort of house I lived in, or the kind of car
I drove. But the world may be different, because I was
important in the life of a child.
—Forest E. Witcraft (1894 – 1967)

THE REASON:

Not In Vain, by Emily Dickinson

If I can stop one heart from breaking,
I shall not live in vain:
If I can ease one life the aching,
Or cool one pain,
Or help one fainting robin
Unto his nest again,
I shall not live in vain.

A portion of the proceeds from this book have been and will be donated to the support of the Hug-a-Tree and Survive *program now managed by the National Association for Search and Rescue (NASAR).* Hug-a-Tree *is a program for children that teaches simple wilderness survival techniques should a child become lost. Anyone interested in the program should visit the NASAR web site (www.nasar.org).*

ACKNOWLEDGEMENTS

The authors wish to acknowledge the assistance and support of everyone who participated in the production of this book, including Roger Bryant, Peggy Fisher, Guy Kotch, Penny Brockman, John Cole Mills, Lillian Cooper, and Brian Cooper, who made themselves available when special needs arose. To Judith Gregory, our loving thanks for, during the writing of the first edition, performing the literary equivalent of turning moose feces into rose petals. She is talented, diplomatic and kind.

The first edition of this book could not have been finished without the continuing support of Rick LaValla and Skip Stoffel, who helped with everything from editing to the arduous process of making it all just right. They both helped without concern for personal gain and in exchange only for the knowledge that this important information would be disseminated and the significant legacy of Ab Taylor's work would be available to our descendants.

We would also like to acknowledge the hard work and dedication of trackers all over the world who use their skill to help others. Their willingness to aid those in need is encouraging in these times when helping others is often relegated to saints and storytellers. There can be no finer legacy.

To our families, we offer both gratitude and apologies. Gratitude for allowing us to pursue what we believe is important and for granting us the encouragement as well as the solitude, whichever was required, to follow through with such a time-consuming task. Apologies for the time, a most precious commodity, when we had to be working, but would rather have been elsewhere.

To Lillian Taylor, whose constant, loving assistance allowed this book to be completed, our fondest regards. By some means, she was able to hold down her husband long enough for him to complete his work in spite of himself. In this way, Lillian has done more to support tracking education across the U.S. than perhaps anyone else. Not only did she undertake the unenviable task of seeing that Ab made it to classes on time, she kept Ab happy, even when he was sober. God bless this special lady.

Finally, a very special thanks to Ken Taylor who, after a significant loss, helped assure that any depiction of Ab's personal life and history was as accurate and true as possible.

To you all, we offer our sincerest thanks.

TABLE OF CONTENTS

FOREWORD TO THE THIRD EDITION

For those of you who do not know Albert "Ab" Taylor, please allow me to take you on a brief tour of his life and career so you might better understand why he was so special.

Albert Snow Taylor, 1924 – 2013. Photo taken circa 1985.

Albert Snow Taylor was born in San Angelo, Texas, on November 24, 1924. After a long, colorful life of caring and contribution, he died on September 9, 2013, in Alpine, California.

Growing up, Ab worked on his uncle's farm and grandfather's ranch in Texas. He was so eager to enlist in the military during WWII that, before he was old enough, he dropped out of high school and traveled to England where he worked as a civilian aviation mechanic for Boeing repairing B-17 bombers. Although some credit Ab and his colleagues with keeping the 8th Air Force operational at a critical time in world history, Ab was more inclined to defer recognition to the courageous pilots and crews that repeatedly climbed into the aircraft he fixed to make another run. When he was old enough to enlist, Ab returned to the U.S. and served in the Navy from 1941 to 1945. During much of his enlistment, he worked aboard the aircraft carrier *Hancock* (CV-19) in the Pacific under Admiral McCain. He also took up boxing and won Golden Gloves and similar championships. Ab was on the *Hancock* when a kamikaze attacked it in 1945 and sixty-seven of his shipmates died. He was also on the *Hancock* in Japanese waters when the atomic bombs were dropped that ended the war. After the war, Ab returned home, finished high school, met his first wife Ruth Coulter, and enrolled in college. He wanted to be a large-animal veterinarian—he loved animals—until he learned all that entailed ("I have to put my hand where...!?").

In 1949, Ab joined the U.S. Border Patrol at College Station, Texas. He was eventually stationed in Brawley, San Bernardino, Indio, Chula Vista, and ultimately El Cajon, California, where he rose to the position of Senior Agent in Charge. In the 1960s, Ab developed the "Step-by-Step" method of teaching tracking. This simple, systematic approach took the mystery out of teaching tracking and forever removed it from the realm of "magic." Lois Clark McCoy of the San Diego Mountain Rescue Team (SDMRT) recognized the value of tracking in lost person searches and was the first to encourage Ab to train search and rescue (SAR) personnel in the art. This was the start of Ab spending many years teaching thousands of SAR and law enforcement personnel how to track—a feat which, when he finally reached the pearly gates, no doubt easily made up for any of his other "minor" infractions.

In 1967, two days after the murders, Ab tracked the killers of Border Patrol Agents Theodore Newton and George Azrak to a cabin where the officers' bodies were found. In 1980, a movie called "Borderline" (starring Charles Bronson, Ed Harris, and Bruno Kirby) was loosely based on Ab's career in the Border Patrol and included a plot based on the Newton/ Azrak tragedy. Besides having a brief cameo in the film, Ab served as the technical advisor and gained the respect of many entertainers, as well as his peers, for his work.

In 1975, Ab's first wife, Ruth Evelyn, died of cancer, leaving behind their three children Ken, Stuart and Patti.

Before he retired in 1979, Ab spent over 30 years in the U.S. Border Patrol doing many things, "...most of which can't be discussed in a wholesome work like this," as he put it. However, he spent most of his career near the Mexican border in Southern California tracking countless immigrants trying to pass undetected into the United States. This was well before the existence of today's sophisticated heat and motion sensing technology now in use by U.S. Customs and Border Protection. Ab did it the old fashioned way: he got down on the ground and used his senses to seek and discover small bits of sign, then used these discoveries to track the person who made them. Indeed, he claimed to receive the most satisfaction from the toughest challenges, including tracking murderers, drug traffickers, kidnappers, escaped convicts, smugglers, and lost children. Or, as Richard Louv, a San Diego journalist, once put it, Ab was "the tracker of countless men, a few women, and more than a few children."

Ab teaching Hug-a-Tree, circa 1985.

After meeting his second wife, Dorothy Wagoner, and at the urging of Lois Clark McCoy, Ab became involved in the National Association for Search and Rescue (NASAR), where he eventually served as an instructor and on their board of directors. He was a cherished speaker at NASAR conferences and his presentations were regularly the best-attended. In 1984, Ab received the Hal Foss Award, NASAR's most prestigious award, for his outstanding contributions to the association and the field of search and rescue at the national level.

Ab's life was changed forever after his participation in the search for 9-year-old Jimmy Beveridge in 1981 on Palomar Mountain, near San Diego. After three days of searching, Jimmy's grandfather called Ab, a well-known tracker, to help. Four hundred searchers worked tirelessly for a total of four days looking for Jimmy—before finding his body. He had fallen down a steep slope and likely died of hypothermia. Ab was devastated and said this was the first time in his career he had not found a child he was tracking. Shortly after this, Ab worked with Jacquie Beveridge, Jimmy's mom, using materials borrowed from Leslie "Grit" Peterson, to develop the "Hug-a-Tree and Survive" program. This child survival program teaches children how to stay safe in the wilderness should they become lost. Ab's 12-year old grandson, Jon (Ken's son), "starred" in the photographic slides initially used to present the program, which were taken by Joe O'Dell of the SDMRT. Tom Jacobs helped with the scriptwriting and educational elements of the program. In 2004, after hundreds of Hug-a-Tree presentations and decades of work on the program, Ab turned the Hug-a-Tree program over to NASAR to manage and maintain. In 2007, proceeds from the first editions of this book and NASAR's FUNSAR book helped provide the resources to develop a new Hug-a-Tree instructional video and improve the printed materials. Hundreds of Hug-a-Tree presenters have in the past, and still to this day, teach this program in the U.S. and around the world, and it has been directly responsible for the successful outcome of thousands of search incidents where lost children might not have survived but for its teaching.

In the late 1980s, Ab traveled around the country in his motor home with his third wife, Lillian Beam. Hundreds of times they led two-day tracking seminars and made Hug-a-Tree presentations, and I had the pleasure of

Ab in 1995.

joining them on dozens of these trips. Without exception, I learned something new every time Ab spoke—often that the story I heard at the previous seminar had changed a bit (grin), but also about how to become a better tracker.

After many years of following Ab around and documenting his techniques, wisdom and stories, Ab allowed me to help him share his methods in a book. Thus, in 1990, we published the first edition of the "Fundamentals of Mantracking" book, with the help of our mutual friends at the Emergency Response Institute in Washington State, Rick LaValla and Skip Stoffel.

Ab believed and taught that experience is the best teacher when it comes to tracking. This is one reason he disliked terms like "expert," "advanced" or even "good" tracker. He believed everyone who aspired to be a tracker was constantly learning, not only from hard work and practice—and it takes a great deal of practice—but also from mistakes. Ab told the story of a Border Patrol newbie who asked, as he pointed to a clear impression of a cattle hoof on the ground near the Mexican border, "How can you possibly know that was made by a person who cut off and strapped a steer's hooves to his feet?" Ab responded in a fatherly voice, "Well, my boy, we just don't see too many two-legged heifers in this part of the country. You'd have to go a bit closer to where you're from for that."

I could go on, but I do not want anyone to feel that Ab was superhuman. He was not. As a matter of fact, his down-to-earth manner and approachability were among his main charms. He was a regular, passionate guy who just wanted to help and could not bear to see a child suffer. He was also a tough, gruff, straight-talking, bow-legged rascal. He could curse, swear, argue and fight with the worst, then bare a tender, compassionate side when someone needed help. He could tell a story better than Mark Twain, drink beer with any type of crowd, and tried to mix the two whenever possible. He indeed was, and will always be fondly remembered as, one-of-a-kind.

He knew he would never get rich from what he brought to others—that is, if you count your fortunes in cash. Indeed, Ab enjoys riches too few of us will ever know: the gratitude of families that might not have their loved ones but for him—a legacy of which to be proud, and very few can match. His friends of faith believe he is now forever reaping the benefits of his earthly contributions and sacrifices.

Why am I telling you all this? Well, when the early editions of this book were drafted, Ab was a great-grandfather and getting on in years. Even then, but more so now, I cannot bear the thought that anyone interested in SAR might not have a chance, as I have, to enjoy and benefit from his teaching. Further, I believe that how information is conveyed is as important, if not more so, than the information itself, and delivery is where Ab shined. I can teach tracking, Ab told me—always with a touch of sarcasm in his voice—as can many others; but none of us will ever match the almost mythical uniqueness of the legendary Ab Taylor. I want aspiring trackers, through this book, to be able to hear what Ab has to say; in his words, in his way. I want everyone to understand that, as with thousands of trackers in the U.S. and abroad, what I know about tracking, I learned from Ab.

This book is a chance for me to document Ab's thoughts and words on basic tracking and convey them to others so they might get a feel for what it was like to hear it from him.

My role is, as honestly as possible, to narrate his teachings; to convey to others what I was privileged to learn from him. If this book fails to convey its message, it can only be my fault for not seeing that the content accurately reflects how Ab taught. If the message comes through, Ab deserves the credit for seeing that I didn't screw it up.

I am honored that Ab felt me worthy of committing his thoughts, ideas and methods to paper. I also think you are privileged, as many of us have been, to have this opportunity to learn from him. I encourage you to use your knowledge as Ab did: to help others. Perhaps you, too, might enjoy the same break Ab undoubtedly has at the pearly gates.

Cheers,
Donald C. Cooper

AB'S PREFACE TO THE FIRST AND SECOND EDITIONS
(SUBTITLE: IT'S MY BOOK AND I CAN DO AS I DAMN WELL PLEASE!)

I thought I would take this opportunity to convey a few thoughts. For you disbelievers: yes, I do have thoughts, and occasionally they impress even me. For you who know better, sit down and listen up anyway.

As you read through this book, I would ask that you please excuse my "French." Hell, "French" is how I've always talked. And, right or wrong, I'm too old now to clean up my act. My associates (Cooper, LaValla, Stoffel) have attempted to soften my direct quotes, but those of you who are familiar with those "gentlemen" may wonder what they know about decency, anyway. At any rate, any "French" spoken here is not intended to offend. So, those of you who might be offended by such things can do two things, only one of which will make it past the censors: stop reading now.

Now, I want to immediately point out two truths regarding this book. The first is that, without question, the person most responsible for mantracking as a useful search technique today is Lois Clark McCoy. Lois had faith—and a vision.

Whether through ignorance or innocence, she believed that all volunteers could be taught to be track aware. She gave me no peace until I eventually realized the full dedication of search and rescue personnel. Ultimately, we learned that a few would actually become very skilled and effective trackers. I hesitate to say "good trackers" because I tend to be very cautious about classifying degrees of tracking skills. I guess this is because I have seen some pretty sorry trackers, who looked and acted the part, and even happened to find a thing or two with easy tracking and quite a bit of luck. (*Look out – this is where the subtitle comes from.*) The scenario goes like this: This self-proclaimed tracker, who actually found a child once on a search, becomes known as the resident "expert" and conveys the same to his peers. No one is called into an area until ole "Ned" has first crack at it. The real problem only becomes evident when nearly 200 searchers follow ole "Ned" for two days on the wrong tracks because several hundred Boy Scouts with the same size foot happened to be in the same area. Worse, "Ned" didn't know that the boy's mother originally stated that the child was wearing tennis shoes only because she was embarrassed to tell anyone that he only had one pair of shoes, which he was wearing, and they were actually dress shoes (with heels). But that's not all. On the first day of the search, "Ned" disregarded a single set of child's tracks, two miles from camp, going away from where the rest of the children were. After all, the track had a heel and he was looking for a flat shoe.

As you might have expected, this is a true story. The boy was eventually found, but not by "Ned" and, unfortunately, not alive. This is just one excruciating example of the results of acquiring a title and responsibility without the years of experience and dedication necessary to justify it. Worse, no one seemed to even know that one lucky day does not make an expert. It takes a track record (pun intended), a history, and a lot of mistakes. You cannot read one book, add ego, stir in some ignorance, and come up with a tracker. No, this sounds more like the ingredients of an incident commander to me.

Realistically, a very small percentage (I'd say less than 1%) of tracking students will have, or will take, the time and dedication to become good trackers. Fortunately, it is not necessary for everyone to be a great tracker in a search. It is far more important that EVERY searcher become *track aware*. Track aware searchers using the Step-by-Step system with other standard SAR techniques <u>will</u> be successful. This is the thrust of my entire rambling message: **Become track aware!**

A real mystery to me is why "expert" trackers make learning to track so complicated. Maybe it's ego, or perhaps a desire to limit the competition. The most complicated part of tracking is that it's tedious. Contrary to what you may believe based on Hollywood's portrayal of the skill, tracking can be very boring and it requires rigid discipline, particularly while you are learning. Most people just don't have the patience or time to become proficient at it.

I guess I could impress folks by, when teaching tracking, making up some new words like "64 points of separation" or "1000 points of light"—both of which you will see when a horse kicks you in the head or you get hit with a 2-by-4—but neither will teach you much about finding the next track. What they will teach you is to be alert around horses asses—whether 2- or 4-legged.

On a search, what I usually see is these hero-types running around burning up energy, gas, and time making noise and great clouds of dust doing things that make sense only to them, some search bosses, and all news media folks. Now, the poor little kid may never be found, and certainly not quickly. After this great adrenaline circus wears down and reaches a manageable level, then intelligence, logic, and reason can be applied to the problem and a systematic search can be run. Then, and only then, can the tracker begin his methodical system of search, provided there are any of the victim's tracks left. And this, children, is the biggest mystery in search and rescue. Why are mantrackers always thought of last, after we see if the victim can be found fast or easy? I guarantee that if you've tried fast and easy, then the tracker is going to find it slow and hard.

Alright, enough of my sniveling. You are probably thinking, "so what the hell was that other truth?" Standby. Here it is: I didn't write this book, Don Cooper did. The fact that you are reading this is an amazing feat, and it's all due to years of patient persistence by Don. He chose to tackle the challenge of extracting 30 years of accumulated knowledge from my head by being a pain in the other end. To his credit, he never gave up, and, somehow, he knew just how hard to push to balance my guilt from nonperformance with my complete annoyance of him. He is now immanently qualified to be a proctologist.

I never wanted, nor did I think it possible, to teach tracking with a book. Maybe it's because of all the complicated B.S. I see coming out as gospel from alleged "expert" trackers. I think it's time for someone to try to bring the skill back into the realm of reality.

I do not enjoy writing or sitting around for long periods of time unless actively involved in either fishing or drinking beer. So, dear readers, please approach this monumental effort with some degree of tolerance and sympathy and realize that any work product was very painfully extracted from me over a long period of time by a miserable little amateur proctologist (DC).

This book will not make you able to track an ant across a granite boulder, but it should help advance you beyond an introductory level if read with an open mind.

Thanks for listening. Enjoy!

—**Ab, 1990**

INTRODUCTION

Tracking can be very effective in law enforcement situations involving burglary, murder, rape, terrorism, and more. But, a tracker will get no more satisfaction from practicing his or her art than can be achieved from its use in finding a lost or missing person. For this reason, and because most basic tracking skills are similar, the primary focus of this book will be tracking within search and rescue situations. This does not mean, however, that the same skills cannot be used to solve crimes. We just prefer describing tracking in a more positive light that does not always involve unsavory types.

In writing this book, there are certain presumptions we, the authors, have made for you, the reader.

First, we presume that you are involved in search and rescue (SAR), law enforcement or, at least, have an interest in them. Any involvement in SAR, law enforcement, military, security or related activities would enhance one's understanding of the material and would make learning much easier. While the information addressed in this book is basic in nature, some terminology and certain ideas may be confusing to those uninitiated in the fundamentals of SAR and/or law enforcement. We recommend, therefore, that some exposure to these topics be sought before attempting to put the

> You didn't jump from your mother's womb to running a race, and neither can you expect to be a tracker after one day with me.
>
> – Ab Taylor

concepts in this text to work. The National Association for Search and Rescue (www.nasar.org) may be a good place to start with the educational process.

Basically, we want the reader to know what tracking is, to develop an interest in becoming involved, and to have a place to practice what is learned.

Second, we want you to understand that this text will not teach the reader tracking. This text is designed to offer information that can be used to supplement a complete tracking program taught by competent instructors. Further, we believe that tracking is not something that can be taught through a book at all. Books like this, as well as most tracking instructors, exist simply to offer the tools a motivated individual requires to teach him- or herself tracking. The real teacher of tracking is experience. We hope that any reader of this work will understand that experience must accompany knowledge gained from reading. Those with a real burning desire to learn tracking can dedicate many hours, days, months, and years for training and practice to do well what very few can claim. Both basic and advanced tracking skills are needed in SAR, but only the fundamentals are discussed in this book.

We have dispensed with much of the detail that other books on tracking have included in an attempt to impress less with wordiness than with clarity. Much more can be taught with regard to tracking than we have included in this book, but nothing important to the basic field worker has been left out. You can learn more by using this text in combination with a good tracking course, taught by a qualified instructor, than can be learned from any book alone.

> **If you are not tracking, you are not giving the victim the best chance to survive.**
> — Ab Taylor

Here, we have attempted to break the basics of tracking down into simple, clear concepts that can be understood by any SAR or law enforcement worker. Our goal is to pass basic information on to as many individuals as possible so that, eventually, everyone gets the idea that anyone can track. All it takes is learning the basics, dedication, perseverance, and practice. Hopefully, this book might help, too.

Albert "Ab" Taylor
Donald C. Cooper

CHAPTER 1

TRACKING IN PERSPECTIVE

Tracking, by simple definition, is following signs of track left by someone or something. It is used to detect the path (direction, movement) of someone or something. However, tracking, when applied to SAR missions, becomes a more complex skill. It now not only concerns itself with detection, but with interpretation of clues as well. Tracking is both an investigative (strategy) and an operational (tactics) SAR tool.

> **SAR = Search and Rescue**

> **Sign - any evidence of change from the natural state that is inflicted on an environment by a person's or animal's passage.**

Unfortunately, tracking is underutilized in SAR situations. More often than not, SAR personnel ignore sign and track because they are unaware of its potential. SAR workers and managers prefer, it seems, literally

> **Tracking is a component of an overall SAR management scheme. Anyone seriously interested in either tracking or SAR management should procure the appropriate reference text(s) and training.**

to walk on the very evidence for which they search while staring at their computers and reference books. A story has been printed on the ground and we, as "track aware" searchers, must discover its existence, then learn to read it. This is not to say that once tracking is applied to SAR situations, every lost subject will be found. Rather, tracking will give the subject a much better chance to survive and it can help to prove (or disprove) that a lost person is within a designated search area.

Reading this manual will not make anyone an expert tracker. Tracking is an acquired skill, and it takes determination, patience, and a willingness to learn. Becoming a highly skilled tracker takes thousands of hours of practice. A high price to pay, but when the consequences involve human life, no investment of time seems enough.

No doubt to you it appeared a mere trampling line of slush, but to my trained eyes every mark upon its surface had a meaning.
– Sherlock Holmes in "A Study in Scarlet"

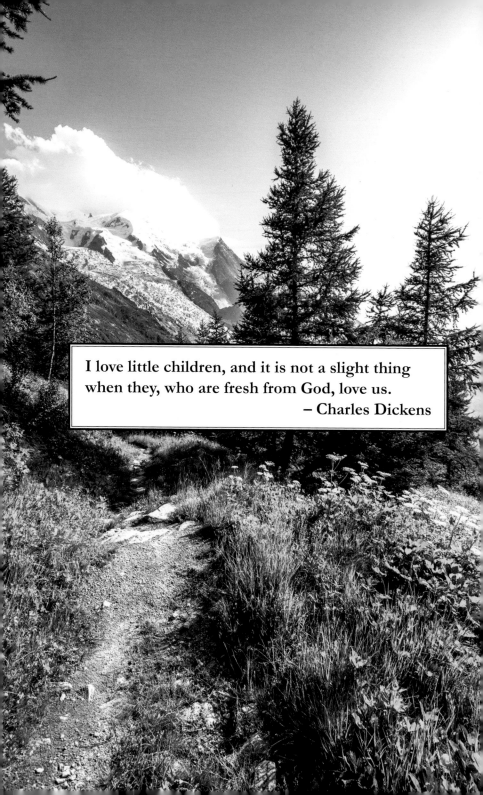

I love little children, and it is not a slight thing when they, who are fresh from God, love us.
— Charles Dickens

CHAPTER 2

WHY TRACK?

In SAR, tracking has many uses. It can be a highly specialized skill that is applied early in a search; it can be used to supplement the existing skills of field searchers; and, tracking training can help make searchers more aware of the possibilities in terms of clues.

Whatever its specific use during an incident, tracking is a valuable and effective method of enhancing the operation and management of any SAR situation.

Consider the potential of a lost subject that can travel 2 mph. If direction of travel is unknown, but a last known point has been determined, the subject could have traveled from that point in any direction and the size of the theoretical search area would look like the one described in the table below:

Travel Time	Travel Distance	Theoretical Search Area
1 hour	2 miles	12.6 square miles
2 hours	4 miles	50.3 square miles
3 hours	6 miles	113.1 square miles

Theoretical Search Area

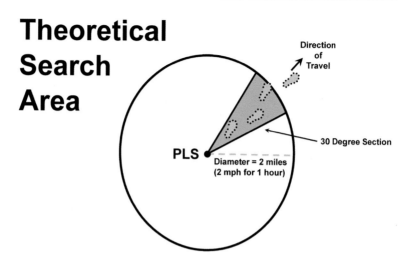

If a clue is found, the search area is substantially reduced. As few as three consecutive tracks could indicate the direction of travel.

Imagine the effect on search planning/management of being able to determine the direction of travel by using tracking to find the first few footprints. If, as in the example above, the initial theoretical search area has a 2-mile radius, the total possible search area is quite large. However, the area of a 30-degree section of the total area that reflects the direction of travel is far smaller and more manageable. When tracking is used as an initial resource, the search area is substantially reduced and other resources—usually at a premium—can be more efficiently applied by an astute SAR manager. Isn't it worth investing 30 or 40 minutes at the last known point to eliminate 85% of the potential search area?

Initially, tracking can be used effectively to find clues. When prints have not yet been discovered, searching for a starting point from which to track is sometimes called "sign cutting" (see Chapter 12). Sign cutting is a type of searching developed by the U.S. Border Patrol (USBP), which emphasizes finding every type of clue, no matter how small or seemingly insignificant. If the subject was at the "point last seen" (PLS) or the "last known point" (LKP), he or she must have left evidence. Sign cutting will find that evidence, if possible, thereby uncovering the first solid evidence of the search.

As an investigative tool, tracking is the best insurance a search manager has to either verify or disprove information obtained from witnesses. In addition, sign cutting may be employed later in a search when new evidence is discovered. Sign can be "cut" around the new evidence in order to determine a direction of travel, or to find new prints from which to track. The idea is to have searchers looking for all evidence, not just certain evidence.

> . . . the ultimate goal in teaching SAR personnel to track . . . is to become track aware. Simply put, we must know enough to, first, look for and recognize evidence; and, second, find and act on it.

This, then, is the ultimate goal in training SAR personnel to track. Not to become an expert, but to become *track aware*—to become aware that it is virtually impossible for a person to pass through an area without leaving substantial evidence of his or her passing. Simply put, we must know enough to, first, look for and recognize evidence; and, second, find and act on it.

In searching, more people is seldom better. Sheer numbers do not guarantee success. Neither do millions of dollars or sophisticated equipment. Even the smallest group of well-trained searchers, under the direction of a skillful search commander, is far superior to a large unwieldy group tearing about the country. In fact, the large, untrained, disorganized groups, all too characteristic of searches done in this country, cost far more lives than they save.

– Ab Taylor

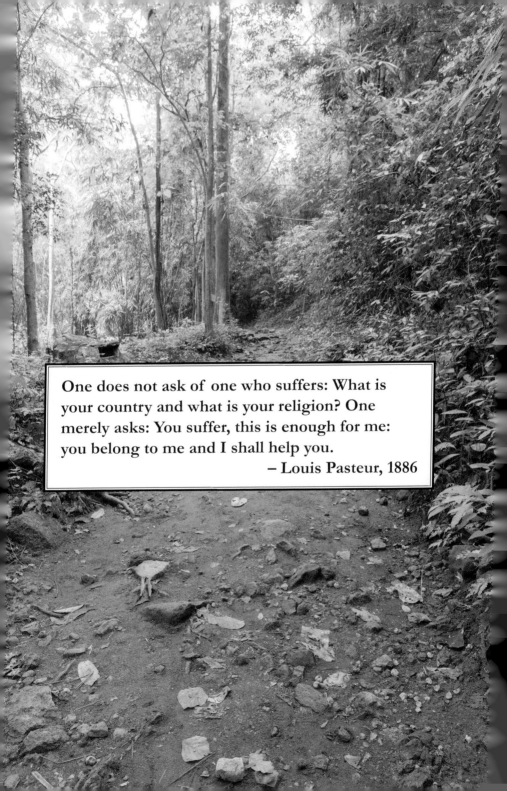

One does not ask of one who suffers: What is your country and what is your religion? One merely asks: You suffer, this is enough for me: you belong to me and I shall help you.

— Louis Pasteur, 1886

CHAPTER 3

HISTORY OF TRACKING IN NORTH AMERICA

Many scientists believe that *Homo erectus*, predecessor of *Homo sapiens*, was the first true "man" to inhabit the earth. A million years before *Homo erectus*, in the late Pliocene or early Pleistocene period, a hominid called *Australopithecus Africanus* (meaning "African southern ape"; AA for short) existed. This creature had an ape-like face, a human-shaped head, a body very similar to modern humans, and it walked erect/upright. AA is important to us because, according to many, it was the earliest of distant human ancestry to leave remnants of tools. These tools lead scientists to believe that AA was a carnivore (meat-eater), which distinguishes it from its predecessors who are believed to have been primarily vegetarians. The fact that AA ate meat indicates that it had to hunt food. Similar to many lower animals, AA most probably used its sense of smell for stalking prey and avoiding enemies. We

> **As some humans became more civilized and began to search for food in the icebox rather than the wilderness, their tracking ability as a survival skill deteriorated.**

can only speculate, but as AA evolved and vision improved, it probably began to notice how prey and enemies would leave evidence of their passing (sign). AA was able to associate this sign with food and began to look for it when hunting. Soon, AA's skills at tracking developed into a valuable survival tool, and smell was used less and less to follow prey and avoid enemies. Tracking, then it seems, could be older than all humankind.

As some humans became more civilized and began to search for food in the icebox rather than the wilderness, their tracking ability as a survival skill deteriorated. It never completely disappeared, however, and we know of frequent use of tracking in North America as recently as in the mid-1800s by native Americans and their contemporaries. This common use in the middle to late 19th century also diminished as more "civilized" methods of food procurement were employed by North American settlers.

Before the early 1900s, the last trackers in America were probably the Native American scouts often employed by the U.S. Cavalry. These mystical characters were vividly depicted in movies as quiet, magical, and never wrong. From one mark on the ground, a "Hollywood" scout could tell you everything from who had made the mark (including their family tree) to the position of the stars when the person passed by. Hollywood's portrayal of these last practitioners of a dying art is firmly embedded in the memories of anyone who has ever watched a classic American "western" movie, but its accuracy is questionable at best. Our present mythical regard for tracking is based in the portrayal of the trackers of that era, but occasionally some truths filtered through. Entertaining movies have taught us that the natives and early settlers of North America used tracking to follow each other. They used footprints and other sign on trails and such areas to determine the whereabouts of their friends as well as their enemies. Both natives and settlers relied on evidence of tracks to indicate if game was available and how plentiful it was. As the need for such skills lessened, however, so did the trackers themselves.

Perhaps the last remnants of tracking skills in the early 1900s in America were found in the western United States, where cattlemen and cowboys had to find, follow, and corral their animals from large open ranges. Fence technology as well as other methods of manipulating animals improved quickly and threatened to relegate the art of tracking to a few ancient practitioners. And worse, the few with the unusual skill would be out of work due to increased technology and the dawn of the machine age.

> **Most people are amazed to learn that tracking is performed every day in the United States by people who are paid to do it.**

Most people are amazed to learn that tracking is performed every day in other countries and cultures as well as by people who are paid to do it in the United States. This relatively forgotten art is practiced daily by members of the

U.S. Border Patrol (now part of U.S. Customs and Border Protection or CBP), primarily at selected stations near the southern border of the U.S., to apprehend aliens who try to enter the U.S. illegally. In 1911, the cattlemen and cowboys that had used tracking for their ranching duties, began applying what they knew to their new jobs in the U.S. Border Patrol. Although most members of today's CBP are not expert trackers, a solid core have been following sign through difficult terrain to track aliens for many years, maintaining skills that might have disappeared otherwise. It is estimated that, from 1960 to 1969, the U.S. Border Patrol El Cajon Station apprehended nearly 60% of the 1000-3000 illegal aliens per month through the use of tracking. Today, the largest, most skilled pool of (professional) trackers in the world could very well exist in the U.S. Border Patrol.

Tracking, as used in search and rescue in the U.S., is based primarily on the efforts of a few Border Patrolmen from the El Cajon Station in Southern California, initially lead by Ab Taylor, and working with the San Diego Mountain Rescue

> In terms of the Border Patrol in the 50s and 60s, I'm considered civilized. Imagine that....
> – Ab Taylor

Team. In the early 1970s, Ab and his colleagues realized that if tracking could help find elusive aliens, it could also be used to find lost persons. Ab and several other Border Patrolmen began volunteering their off-duty time to train SAR personnel in the skills that they have fine-tuned over many years of practice. The training program that evolved from these efforts became known as the *Step-by-Step Method.*

There is a little story written on the ground. Not a fairy tale, a story. Read it to me. – Ab Taylor

The Step-by-Step Tracking Method has become known as the fastest, most effective method to teach tracking to people in a relatively short time. For the past four decades, a major effort has been underway to teach the Step-by-Step Method to SAR personnel so they become more conscious of clues (sign) and, therefore, become better searchers. It is a sad fact that SAR personnel destroy more evidence during a search than they discover. Most believe that if searchers were simply conscious of the possible clues and aware that sign (discoverable evidence) existed, searchers could be far more effective. We refer to this as teaching searchers to be "clue conscious" and "track aware"—two important goals of the Step-by-Step Method and all relevant SAR training.

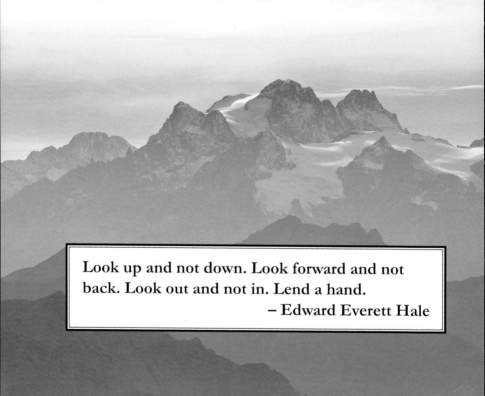

Look up and not down. Look forward and not back. Look out and not in. Lend a hand.

— Edward Everett Hale

CHAPTER 4

WHEN AND WHERE TO USE TRACKING

It cannot be overemphasized that tracking is best utilized in the early stages of a search when evidence (sign/clues) is least contaminated by well-meaning, anxious searchers. Early application of trackers also allows them to find the evidence as soon as possible, possibly preserving some of its time- and weather-sensitive components.

Tracking can also be used as a search progresses. All searchers can utilize tracking and the awareness that it entails to find clues. Any enhancement of clue consciousness by searchers will improve a search and increase the number of successes.

Can tracking be useful in all environments? What about while it's raining? How about at night? No one blanket

> **Evidence is something capable of being presented legally before a court, such as an object or witness, which bears on or establishes a point in question. In tracking, sign and track are considered evidence.**

> **All searchers can utilize tracking and the awareness that it entails to find clues.**

statement can cover all situations where tracking may be used. Sometimes it will be possible to track in the rain and sometimes it will not. Each situation, and each tracker, is different. Consider, however, that an experienced tracker can detect sign that many could not see, and much of this sign could endure a driving rain or a snowy night. A complete print is not always the only evidence of human passage. Depending on the environment, a tracker may look for bent grass, broken twigs, flattened soil, disturbed brush, compressed stones, and many other pieces of evidence that may not be affected by inclement weather. A skilled tracker will improvise. If one approach does not work, he or she

Beautiful prints like this cannot be expected in all terrains.

will try another. If rain has washed away a good print, other evidence may still be discoverable.

Since weather does not necessarily preclude the use of tracking, how about difficult terrain or highly traveled areas? The same principle applies. Let the tracker decide when and where tracking can be effective. Having a non-tracker decide whether tracking will work is like having a house painter

> **Poor weather does not preclude the use of tracking.**

decide whether or not surgery is required. Trackers look for, and often find, sign that frequently eludes the untrained searcher. Even the most difficult terrain can produce a clue that might eventually lead to establishing a direction of travel or locating the subject of the search.

> **Having a non-tracker decide whether tracking will work is like having a painter decide whether or not surgery is required.**

Children, you are very little,
And your bones are very brittle;
If you would grow great and stately,
You must try to walk sedately.

– Robert Louis Stevenson,
"Good and Bad Children"

CHAPTER 5
DEFINITIONS AND TERMINOLOGY

A "track" or "print" is an impression left from the passage of a person that can be positively identified as being human. Further, a track may be complete, meaning that the entire impression is visible; partial, meaning that it is not visible in its entirety; and/or identifiable, meaning that, complete or partial, it has at least one characteristic that differentiates it from others similar to it. "Tracking" is simply defined as following someone, or something, by stringing together a continuous chain of their sign. "Sign" is any evidence of change from the

TERMINOLOGY LIST:
Track or Print -----
    Complete
    Partial
    Identifiable
Tracking -----
    Step-by-Step
    Jump Tracking
    Bracketing
Sign -----
    Conclusively Human
    Corroborant
Sign Cutting -----
    Track Trap
    Cuttable Area

natural state that is inflicted on an environment by a person's passage. A track, whether complete or partial, is many individual pieces of sign combined in such a way as to form a print. The technique is first to find some sign, then interpret it, and ultimately act on it. Simply put, tracking is the ability to discover and combine sign in chronological order, consider its meaning after investigation, and do this over a large area.

In order to be of any use, sign must be discovered. Seeing it is usually fairly easy because there is so much of it. A walking person leaves sign approximately every 18-20 inches, or over 3000 times per mile, so catching even a small percentage of it shouldn't be much trouble. The problem lies not in finding sign, but in determining which is relevant and which is not. The novice tracker, for example, often sees plenty of relevant sign, yet disregards it because he or she thought it to be insignificant. The experienced tracker sees the same information but has learned to glean its meaning.

If sign is considered evidence, then common law enforcement terms can be applied to distinguish different types. Sign can be separated into two categories: conclusively human, and corroborant. "Conclusively human" sign is a disturbance, which, on its own, can positively be said to have been caused by a person and not an animal. The use of the "SAFE" test (see box on following page) can be helpful in determining if a print is conclusively human. "Corroborant" sign is disturbance that is not decisively human and could have been caused by an animal. This type of sign may corroborate other

---

A walking person leaves sign about every 18 to 20 inches, or over 3000 times per mile.

evidence but, when considered on its own, is not conclusive. It cannot be positively determined to have been caused by a person, but may confirm or substantiate other evidence with which it may be found.

THE "SAFE" TEST
(How to determine if a print is human):
S –   **Is it the size and shape of a human print?**
A –   **Does it include one or more 90 degree angles?**
F –   **Is there significant flatness, especially in the size and shape of a human print?**
E –   **Does it have one or more clear edges that incorporate sharp or 90 degree angles?**

"Sign cutting" is looking for sign in order to establish a starting point from which to track. Tracking involves following a chronology of sign, or consecutive tracks, step-by-step. Sign cutting is searching for the first sign or track. Another principal difference between tracking and sign cutting is that tracking is done by traveling the same direction as the person who laid the track; sign cutting is done traveling (ideally) perpendicular to the direction of travel of the person being followed. Sign cutting is done by looking for sign in a path that would intersect that of the person who laid the track. It is most effective when performed in an area where the sign being sought is most visible and easily seen. An area that is particularly good for finding sign, such as wet sand, mud, soft dirt or snow, is sometimes called a "track trap" or "cuttable" area. Track traps can also be man-made by scraping an area clean so as to show sign easily.

Sign cutting can substantially reduce the search area by detecting sign that indicates direction of travel. This can be a very efficient application of resources, particularly at the onset of an incident when urgency is high and the quantity of searchers/trackers is low.

"Jump tracking" is a form of tracking that involves finding a big, obvious footprint, then proceeding along the presumed direction of travel until another obvious track is found. Jump tracking involves guesswork, luck, essentially no skill, and can be dangerous when a life depends on skillful tracking. One of the biggest problems in tracking has always been the destruction of sign by unknowing, energetic, and well-meaning searchers. Jump tracking offers great potential for this type of clue erasure. Since virtually all humans can jump track without training, this is not the type of tracking that will be discussed here.

Although there are multiple ways to describe it, in this book "stride" is the measured distance between the rear margin of the heel of one footfall and the rear margin of the heel of the following footfall. "Step-by-Step tracking" is a disciplined teaching system, where a tracker sees each step in sequence and proceeds no further than the last visible track, using the stride to determine where next to look for sign. This system, above all, makes searchers of all types clue conscious and track aware (aware that track and sign exist). It is the standard for which an experienced tracker will strive at all times. In theory, a tracker will attempt to find every piece of evidence left by his or her quarry. In a real situation, this is not always possible and even the best trackers must accept small gaps in the continuous chain of evidence. The words "small gaps" best distinguish the Step-by-Step Method from jump tracking.

"Bracketing" is an occasionally acceptable method of interpolation between tracks that can be used when standard Step-by-Step approaches fail to produce. Bracketing is meant as a stopgap measure that uses a predetermined stride to skip one step in sequence in order to find the next, and then use it to find the one skipped. In terms of the Step-by-Step approach, bracketing is cheating because it involves moving past the last visible sign in order to continue the track. Bracketing, however, is not a license to jump track and should be used only infrequently to maintain continuity on an important track. Students may come to this on their own but will never receive permission to do it.

Programs that teach the Step-by-Step Method do not teach tracking *per se*. They teach an approach that offers the tools to teach oneself tracking. Anyone can learn to track. All it takes beyond learning the basics of the Step-by-Step approach, if you are motivated, is practice—hours and hours of practice. You may never become an expert tracker; but, at the very least, the Step-by-Step approach will make you track and sign aware and, therefore, a better searcher.

> **Anyone can learn to track, but it takes motivation and practice. Lots and lots of practice.**

Using common terms to describe the various parts of the foot can be useful while tracking. Generally, the "heel" is the back part of the foot below the ankle and the "forefoot" is the larger part of the foot forward of the ankle. "Medial" is a medical term that can often be useful to describe something that is situated toward the middle or midline of the body. "Lateral" is the term used to describe something

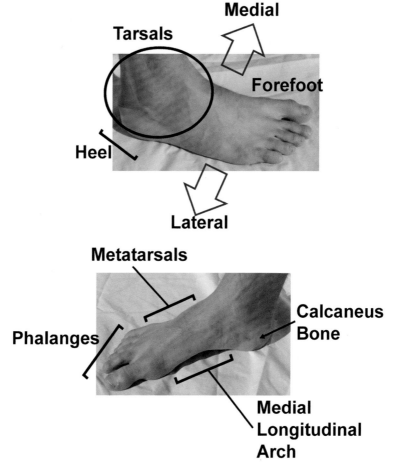

Terms describing parts of the foot.

situated away from the middle or to the side; usually to the left or the right. On most feet, the little toe is lateral and the big toe is medial. The term "anterior" is used to refer to something toward the front of the body or toward the head, and "posterior" is used to describe something toward the back of the body. The "arch" of the foot usually refers to the bottom, medial part of the foot just forward of the ankle that curves above the ground. It stretches from the heel bone (the calcaneus) to the three medial metatarsals (five middle, long bones of the foot). Medical practitioners also refer to this arch as the "medial longitudinal arch." The bones of the toes are called "phalanges," and the big bones of the foot below and including the ankle and the calcaneus are called the "tarsals."

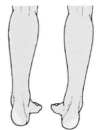

Supination

"Supination" of the foot is a movement of the foot and leg in which the foot rolls outward with an elevated arch so that in walking the foot tends to come down on its outer edge. When the foot falls flat on the ground, striking both the outer edge and inner margin at the same time, this is considered "neutral" movement of the foot. "Pronation" of the foot is rotation of the medial (middle) bones in the midtarsal region of the foot inward and downward so that in walking the foot tends to come down on its inner margin. These terms can be useful when trying to describe how a foot struck the ground to produce a track.

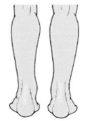

Neutral

Pronation

Common movements of the foot and leg: Supination (top), Neutral (middle) and Pronation (bottom).

The pattern of how a person walks is called "gait" and may vary depending on the medical or physical condition of the subject. "Steppage gait" is when one walks with a foot drop where the foot hangs with the toes pointing down, causing the toes to scrape the ground while walking and requiring the walker to lift the leg higher than normal when walking. "Waddling gait" is a duck-like walk where the lateral distance between footfalls can be larger than a normal gait. The lateral distance between footfalls, perpendicular to the direction of travel, is referred to as "straddle" and can be measured just like stride. Straddle can increase when one carries a heavy load.

When one walks with the toes pointed inward (medially), this is sometimes called "pigeon toed" or "intoeing." In medical terminology, the terms metatarsus varus or metatarsus adductus may be used. The opposite of intoeing is "toe out" or "splayed feet," which is when the toes point outward (laterally) when walking.

Every child comes with the message that God is not yet discouraged of man.

— Rabindranath Tagore

CHAPTER 6

WHAT DOES IT TAKE TO TRACK?

As stated earlier, anyone can learn to track. It simply takes a willingness to learn, patience, determination, hard work, and practice. Not unlike any important endeavor. But, keep in mind; everyone does not have to become a tracking "guru." Just having the interest and open-mindedness to attend a Step-by-Step program will probably improve your value as a searcher. The world does need expert trackers, and everyone with the aforementioned characteristics is strongly encouraged to pursue such a vocation. But take the Step-by-Step training first before deciding to sell everything and live the tracking life. It will offer what most SAR personnel desire by simply making them track aware.

> It doesn't take three generations of Native American blood or sleeping with Davy Crockett to make you a tracker.
>
> – Ab Taylor

QUALITIES OF A GOOD TRACKER

- Patience
- An inquisitive mind
- Honesty – to oneself and others
- Perseverance
- Good observation skills
- Honed senses (all 5)
- Endurance
- Good field craft skills – comfortable in field
- Determination (mental and physical)
- Knowledge of fauna and flora
- Curiosity

EQUIPMENT FOR TRACKING:

1. Appropriate clothing
2. Sign cutting stick
3. Measuring device
4. Notepad and pencil
5. Trail tape
6. Flashlight
7. Mirror
8. Eyes (corrected vision)

Equipment for Tracking

Tracking, essentially, requires very little equipment. A pair of eyes which, aided or not, provide nearly 20/20 vision is tracking's only prerequisite. However, experience has indicated that some items can be quite helpful.

1. CLOTHING should be appropriate for the terrain and weather, and durable enough to withstand ventures into dense brush and rugged terrain. A broad-brimmed hat may be handy for protecting the eyes from the sun, or shading tracks when the sun is high in the sky. Above all, the tracker must be able to work comfortably in whatever environment he or she is thrust.

2. A WALKING OR SIGN CUTTING STICK is a must, especially for novice trackers. A light, durable stick, approximately 40 inches long, is best, but longer may be preferred. This stick, which is used to focus the attention of a tracker, should have at least two "O" rings or rubber bands on it for measuring distance and stride (some trackers use many more than two rings).

3. A MEASURING DEVICE such as a tape measure can be valuable when measuring print size or stride. Some trackers attach a measuring tape to their stick, but most simply carry a metal, carpenter's-type, tape measure in their pocket.

4. A small NOTE PAD and PENCIL are needed to record measurements and fill out track reports. A good drawing of a print will be indispensable.

5. TRAIL TAPE can be carried to cordon off evidence or sign, or to prevent the trampling of a good track. Plastic surveyor's tape works well, but care must be taken to see

that it is retrieved after it has served its purpose. Royal blue is the best color for this purpose.

6. A FLASHLIGHT can be important when light is not at an optimum. Since light plays such an important part in seeing, its easy to appreciate how an artificial light source could be helpful.

7. A MIRROR can be used to redirect natural light low across sign when the sun is high in the sky.

Tracking is not an equipment-intensive pursuit. Sight, patience, perseverance, and determination are the only real requirements to be a tracker. The above-mentioned specific equipment is helpful, but the brain and the body are the primary tools of the trade.

> Oh, how simple it would have been had I been here before they came like a herd of buffalo and wallowed all over it.
> Here is where the party with lodgekeeper came, and they have covered all the tracks for six or eight feet around the body.
>   – Sherlock Holmes in "The Boscombe
>   Valley Mystery"

Credo of the Novice Tracker

The fundamental principle on which tracking is based is sound training. The rules upon which all future tracking experience is based lie within the following credo. These very basic rules also serve as the ABCs of the Step-by-Step Method of tracking.

CREDO OF THE NOVICE TRACKER

1. Do not advance beyond the last print until you find the next one.
2. Do not destroy the evidence.
3. Use a sign cutting stick.
4. See rules 1 and 2.

AB'S PUNISHMENT FOR SIGN DESTRUCTION

1. Forced to sit in the Jeep until your genitals* fall off.
2. Shot on the spot and/or apply the "Texas Hobble" (see page 113).

* paraphrased

Any track or sign is considered evidence until proven otherwise. Treat all track and sign as if it were positively identified as being that of the person being sought. Once a track or sign has been destroyed, it cannot be reconstituted. It is lost forever. The destruction of a track, clue, or any sign not only chips away at the finite body of available information, it reduces the chances of meeting your objective. If that objective is finding a lost person, destroying tracks, clues, or any sign can literally mean the difference between life and death.

Beyond simply finding and interpreting sign, a tracker is obliged to protect it. Remember, any clue is important, no matter how small or seemingly insignificant. Do not move from one place to another without being track aware. An untrained person stepping on good sign or track is unfortunate. A tracker or searcher doing the same is inexcusable.

(a) (b)

(c) (d)

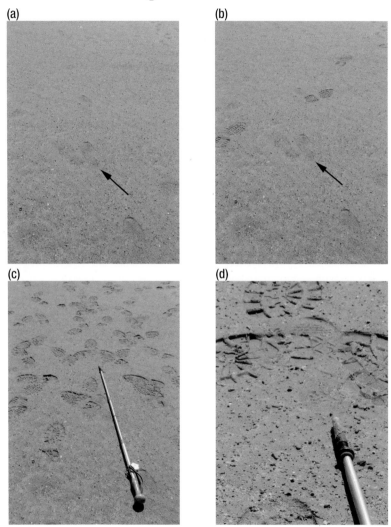

The arrows and tracking stick point to the lost child's track (a). (b) Note untrained searcher's tracks starting to obscure and destroy the child's track. (c) (d) Now, it is much harder and it may be too late for novice trackers to find the child's track.

> **This is my message: Be track aware. Give the victim every chance to survive.**
>
> **– Ab Taylor**

Light

Since tracking is an intensely visual skill, it is easy to see how light plays an important role. Tracking is far simpler when the light is of the proper intensity and from the right direction. However, Mother Nature does not always supply the optimum lighting conditions required for tracking during a SAR incident. When learning to track, using the sun properly is one of the most important things to learn. Tracks are easiest to see when the sun is at a low angle, e.g., early in the morning and late in the afternoon. When the sun is low, it causes longer shadows that bring out the details of any depression on the ground, making sign easier to see. Clouds, diffuse light (through pollution or clouds), and the sun high overhead all diminish the shadow effect. Put simply: Sign and track are usually easier to see while facing the light source, and with that source at a low angle to the ground.

Since facing the light source can make tracks easier to detect, moving around into a position to optimize the angle to the sun is to be encouraged. Be careful, however, that you do not trample evidence in your search for the proper angle from which to view. The angle will not matter if you have nothing to look at but your own footprints.

> **Sign and track are usually easier to see while facing the light source, and with that source at a low angle to the ground.**

Tracking at Night

Because light plays such an important role in tracking, it is easy to see how tracking can be performed at night when the light source is completely under the control of the tracker. An artificial light source can be rotated completely around the track from a low angle to allow for the best view, thus emphasizing otherwise unnoticed sign. An additional benefit of tracking at night can be realized if the lost individual stops moving (to sleep, for instance), thereby allowing night trackers to catch up.

In addition, since darkness at night hides most of the distractive nuances seen during the day, your light source can serve to focus your attention and concentration where it should be.

A diffuse hand lantern works best when tracking at night. Some success has been achieved with Coleman® lanterns with deflectors that keep the light out of the tracker's eyes. Also, battery-powered fluorescent lanterns have been used effectively. The key, however, is not brightness. The flashlights commonly carried by law enforcement personnel that serve as attitude adjusters and fire starters (with light beam only) are generally worthless as tracking lights. These bright lights diminish night vision and are too intense to bring out subtle sign on an otherwise dark night. The ideal night tracking light should not be so bright as to ruin night vision, yet last a long time (good battery life), be light and durable, and offer a diffuse beam.

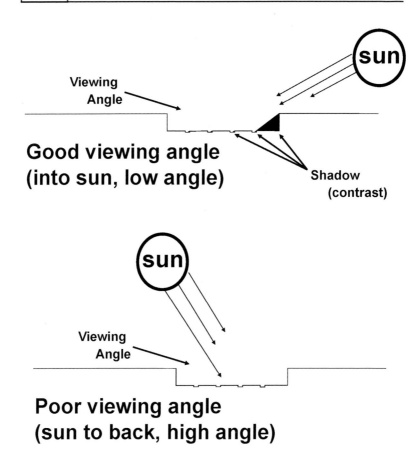

**Good viewing angle
(into sun, low angle)**

**Poor viewing angle
(sun to back, high angle)**

When viewing even the slightest impression on the ground, keep the light source facing you and at a low angle (top) to enhance the use of shadows that contrast and outline details within the track. Viewing with the light at your back or at a high angle (bottom) is far less effective.

Some experienced trackers have attached headlamps to their lower legs, just below the knee, or to their tracking sticks to obtain the best angle while walking. The U.S. Border Patrol often uses lights attached low on a vehicle for cutting sign on a road. The proper light attached at the correct angle can allow a driver, or observer/spotter, to follow track on the side of the road for a great distance at a faster speed than could be achieved on foot.

Be imaginative, and try night tracking yourself. You will be amazed at how well it works.

(a)

(b)

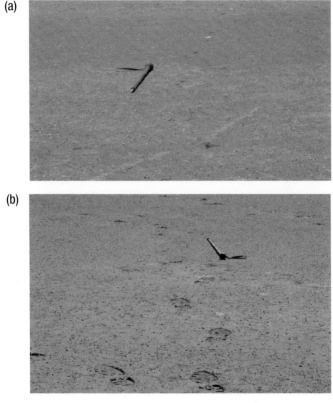

(a) Track viewed in unfavorable light (sun at back, high angle). (b) Same track viewed in more favorable light (sun to front, low angle).

An untrained person stepping on good sign or track is unfortunate. A tracker or searcher doing the same is inexcusable.

This is a print that just happened to fall in a beam of light in a forest, making it easy to see. Sometimes, you just get lucky, but tracking does not depend on luck. It requires hard work, discipline, and practice—lots and lots of practice.

All the beautiful sentiments in the world weigh less than a single lovely action.
— James Russell Lowell

CHAPTER 7

SIGN-CUTTING STICK AND THE STEP-BY-STEP METHOD

O ccasionally something comes "down the pike" that you must see to believe. The sign cutting stick is just such an item.

Most trades have their specialized tools. In tracking, it is the sign cutting stick. It is hard to believe that such a simple tool can be so effective, but it's true. When properly used, a sign cutting stick can seem to make sign pop out of thin air. In reality, all it does is force you to look where you want to be looking, instead of everywhere else.

The Step-by-Step Method of tracking is stride-based. That is, a tracker gets from one track to the next by determining stride (distance from heel of rear print to heel of front

The sign cutting stick causes you to look where you want to be looking, instead of everywhere else.

print), then searching one stride from the last track found. This requires some type of device for measuring stride; for this, the sign cutting stick works well.

When the stride length is indicated on the sign cutting stick by placing the "O" ring or rubber band one stride length from the end, the marker can be placed at the heel of the last track and the end of the stick pointed in the direction of travel. The end of the stick, then, becomes a pointer towards where the next sign or track is expected to be found. The stick causes the tracker's attention to be focused on a small piece of ground rather than a large area. Finding sign is easier when the "search area" is limited. A sign cutting stick does just that.

Measuring stride with a sign cutting stick.

To use the sign cutting stick, do the following:

1. Find or make a stick that is approximately 40 inches long, or longer. On it, place at least two rubber bands (or rubber O-rings) that can be moved on the stick, but will stay in place if desired. For one-time uses, a large twig can be procured from the environment and marked with a knife, pencil, or other marker.

The end of the stick becomes a pointer towards where the next sign or track is expected to be found.

Walking stick used as a sign cutting or tracking stick. Note the orange O-rings used for stride length markers (any band will work) and the attached measuring tape. Any stick will work. It need not be a commercial walking stick like this one. A dowel or limb cut from a tree or bush will work just as well.

2. At the earliest opportunity while tracking someone, determine his or her stride by measuring the distance from the heel of the rear print to the heel on the front print. Position a marker on your sign cutting stick (rubber band, O-rings, or other mark) so that the distance from the tip of the stick to the marker is the same distance as the stride.

3. On the last print found, hold the stick so that the stride mark is held close to, but above, the rear of the heel. Move the tip of the stick through an arc that covers the area where the next track should occur.

4. While sweeping the stick very slowly, study the area directly in front of the tip for sign. Take about twenty seconds to sweep from 10 o'clock to 2 o'clock, focusing primarily to the left for a left print (10 o'clock) or to the

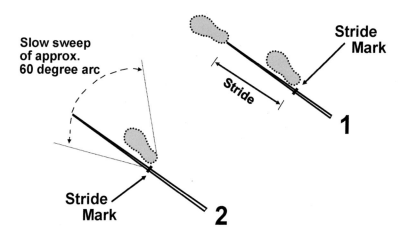

Using the sign cutting stick to find the next sign. (1) Measure a known stride and mark the length with the O-ring or rubber band on the stick (from the tip). (2) Take 20 seconds to sweep from 10 o'clock to 2 o'clock, looking for sign at the tip of the stick. If you don't find anything, make the next sweep even slower and wider.

right for a right print (2 o'clock). Somewhere during the sweep the tip of the stick should be pointing to the heel of the next print. It may be obvious or it may be difficult, but it is there. If you don't find anything during the first sweep, make the next sweep even slower. Constantly be alert to the possibility that the subject being tracked may abruptly change direction or alter his or her stride.

The principles of "vision" are dealt with in some detail in chapter 11, but it is important here to note that a person's eyes are accustomed to wandering as they choose, without the owner/operator being consciously aware of the mechanics involved. Basically, the eyes will do as they please unless directed to do otherwise, which is why we need the assistance of our most valued tool (and friend), the sign cutting stick. This potent tracking aid assists us in training the eye to concentrate on the small piece of real estate, about one square foot, where the next track will fall. As simple as this procedure seems, it is extremely difficult to learn because the eyes are in intimate contact with the brain, which (for most) is capable of performing several functions at once. The eyes, however, are capable of looking only at one spot at a time. While most of us will use and move the stick as we are taught, we too often allow our eyes to nervously dart several steps ahead or to the side, hoping to get lucky and find that big, easy sign (proving that you are related to Daniel Boone after all). The point is this: you are probably cursed with a cheating mind and a wandering eye, and as long as you let them control your actions, you will never learn to track. Force your eyes to return to finding that difficult sign in front of the stick and concentrate there ONLY. This is where you will learn the trade.

Try this exercise: Cut a square out from the middle of a piece of paper, 2 inches by 2 inches, and lay the paper on the ground. Point your sign cutting stick at the square and spend the next 30 minutes or so examining every minute detail within this square. Do you see pebbles or grains of sand? Count them. Note their color, texture, and location within the area. Is there any vegetation in the area? How big? What color? Any insects? What do they look like? You get the idea. Take notes and document everything you learn about this small area, and, after a short break, have your partner repeat the process in the same area. Afterwards, compare notes and learn from each other. This is what sign cutting is all about.

Things can never be as they once were; be sad and rejoice.

– Author Unknown

CHAPTER 8

LABELING TRACKS

It is important when using the sign cutting stick to know if the track being sought is a right footprint or a left one. By marking the last track found, a tracker can immediately tell which (left or right) should be next.

Tracks should be marked in two ways, as shown on the following page: indicate whether they are right or left, and circle them if they are fully identifiable. To mark a track, or partial track, left or right, start by using the sign cutting stick to etch a semicircle to the rear of the track. To a tracker, this arc should indicate that there is a track immediately ahead, STAY OFF. A short hash-mark is placed at the right end of the arc to indicate right, and at the left end of the arc to indicate left.

> **Tracks should be marked in two ways. They should be marked right or left, and they should be circled if they are fully identifiable.**

Trackers are rarely lucky enough to get a series of full prints to follow. They must depend on chaining together a collection of sign. When a print is found that is positively identifiable, that is, there is enough print visible to indicate shoe type and sole pattern, it should be completely encircled. This should indicate to others that they are to stay away so that a drawing can be made and the evidence preserved.

(a) (b)

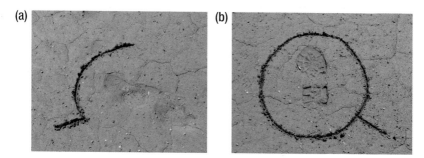

A semicircle indicates that sign is ahead and a hash mark or "tick" at the end of the semicircle denotes a right or left track. Note that the fully identifiable track is completely encircled.

Circle complete, fully identifiable tracks (left). Place a semi-circle behind a partial print with a hash mark on the left to indicate a left print (center) or on the right to indicate a right print (right).

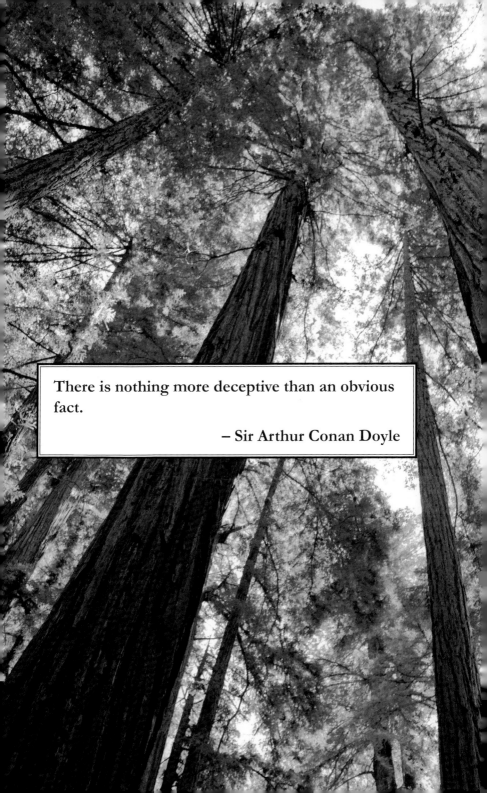

There is nothing more deceptive than an obvious fact.

– Sir Arthur Conan Doyle

CHAPTER 9
DEALING WITH FACTS

It is easy, when attempting to solve a mystery, to search only for solutions that substantiate a preconceived idea or theory. In tracking, trackers search for clues (sign). It can be quite easy to search only for clues that will substantiate a theory that has been developed to explain unanswered questions. Trackers must be careful to deal only with the facts. Search for all clues, not just those that would substantiate a theory.

Be careful not to look for what you think you will find. Look for what is there.

A good example of "tunnel vision" occurred when a tracker tried to figure how much his quarry weighed by comparing the print he was following to his own. He stepped next to the existing print and deduced that his quarry weighed less than he because the fresh print made a deeper impression. One of the possibilities was indeed that the person who made the first track was lighter. However, the fact is that the fresh print was deeper than the old print. That is all. Many explanations could account for the discrepancy. Is the ground softer now? Perhaps the old print had rolled off of a rock, decreasing its impact with the surrounding soil? The point is that the fresh print is deeper; anything further is speculation. Be careful not to confuse the facts with conjecture or speculation. This can lead to searching for clues that fit an erroneous presumption. Worse, it can lead to disregarding sign that is incorrectly deemed irrelevant.

> "It is of the highest importance in the art of detection to be able to recognize, out of a number of facts, which are incidental and which are vital. Otherwise your energy and attention must be dissipated instead of being concentrated."
>
> – Sherlock Holmes from
> Sir Arthur Conan Doyle's
> *The Memoirs of Sherlock
> Holmes* (1984) "The Reigate Puzzle"

When you find yourself tiring or becoming frustrated because you cannot see any sign, rest. Look away for a few minutes. Check out the scenery before returning to what you were doing. Very often, you will now be able see that what was once apparently invisible.

> **When you find yourself tiring or becoming frustrated because you cannot see any sign, rest. Look away.**

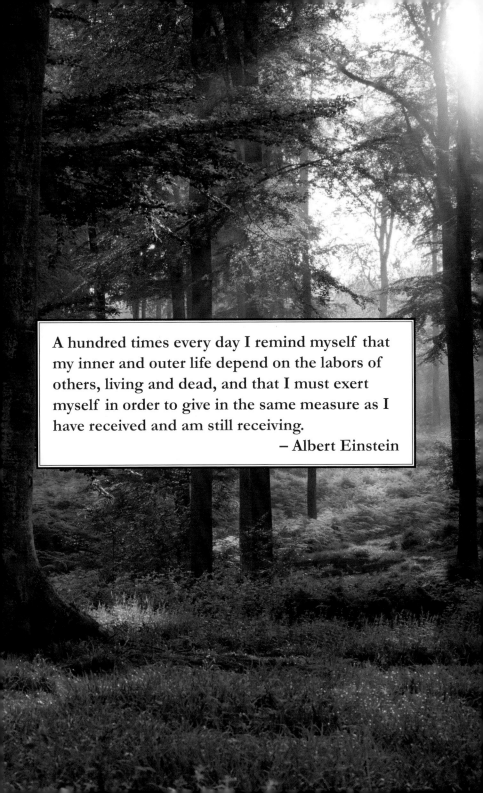

A hundred times every day I remind myself that my inner and outer life depend on the labors of others, living and dead, and that I must exert myself in order to give in the same measure as I have received and am still receiving.

– Albert Einstein

CHAPTER 10
TRACKING TEAM

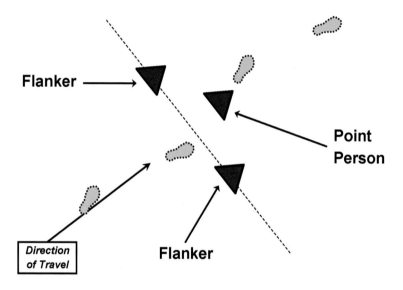

Three-person tracking team. Flankers work on either side, and slightly behind, the Point person. The Point focuses on finding the next track (using the tracking stick) while the Flankers take a wider view.

A common approach to following a track by the Step-by-Step Method is to use three-person teams. The three-person team, comprised of a Point Person and two Flankers, has several advantages:

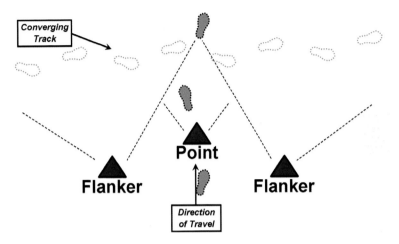

Field of view for three-person tracking team. Flankers look ahead and to the side for converging tracks while the Point concentrates on the area immediately in front of the team.

1. It allows for consultation in difficult situations because three heads are better than one. If you can convince another hard head that what you are seeing is sign, then you are twice as likely to be right.

2. When training, it builds confidence, reduces errors, and benefits students by allowing a verbal exchange of the details of what is seen rather than just mutual observation of a clue.

3. It allows rotation of the Point Person who is physically on the ground searching for sign. Point is a tiring position, especially when sign is limited.

> An interplay of opinion between team members allows ideas that one may have to be filtered through the thoughts of others.

4. It allows the team to split up if several trails diverge. Any team member can call the team back together when one finds that he or she is on the correct track. Actually, this is sign cutting and can lead to bad habits during the learning phase, so be careful.

The general responsibilities of the team members are as follows:

Point

• Stays just behind the last track found, uses a sign cutting stick to search for the next one and mark the tracks as the team progresses.

• Keeps Flankers from obliterating sign by getting ahead and whacks them if they do.

• Coordinates efforts of team.

Flankers

• From more of an upright position, the Flankers watch the side for incoming tracks that might confuse the situation.

• They watch for a sudden turn of the trail being followed.

• They help the Point find the next track from their vantage positions.

Tracking, like other types of searching, is not something that can be done all day long without rest. For a tracker to be effective, he or she must rest at regular intervals and rotate through the Point position with other trackers. Searching for anything while exhausted and fatigued is actually detrimental to the search effort. Sign or track, like all evidence in a search, must be discovered to be useful. Pressing on while fatigued is admirable, but a tired tracker may miss things that could affect the entire effort. When lives may weigh in the balance, this is unacceptable.

> For a tracker to be effective, he or she must rest at regular intervals and rotate through the Point position with other trackers.

A component of the tracking team that is often misunderstood is the continuous exchange of ideas and information that should take place between team members. An interplay of opinion between the Point and Flankers allows ideas that one may have to be filtered through the thoughts of the others. This interaction could be as simple as the Point continuously talking about what is seen, and can include each of the Flankers challenging the Point so that all opinions on any discovery can be considered. After everyone has spoken their piece, a consensus can be achieved. This ends up being an efficient way of preventing an overbearing individual from pushing the team in an undesirable direction. When everyone is involved in what is going on, there is a better chance that the team is heading the right way. Do not construe this to mean that silence is never desirable, however.

> You are 10 times more likely to be right if you can describe what you are seeing to another person and they agree with you.
> – Ab Taylor

Occasionally, when great concentration is required, silence may indeed be golden.

If you take the time to describe, in detail, what you see and why you think it relates to your subject's track, you'll be much less likely to con yourself into moving to the next step without just cause.

During 30 years of tracking clever aliens, I could move at a good walking pace all day long over terrain that seemed to yield very little evidence. When it became necessary for me to describe to new Border Patrolmen what I saw, and why I was sure of what I saw, I reached a substantially improved plateau of tracking competence. There's an important lesson here.

– Ab Taylor

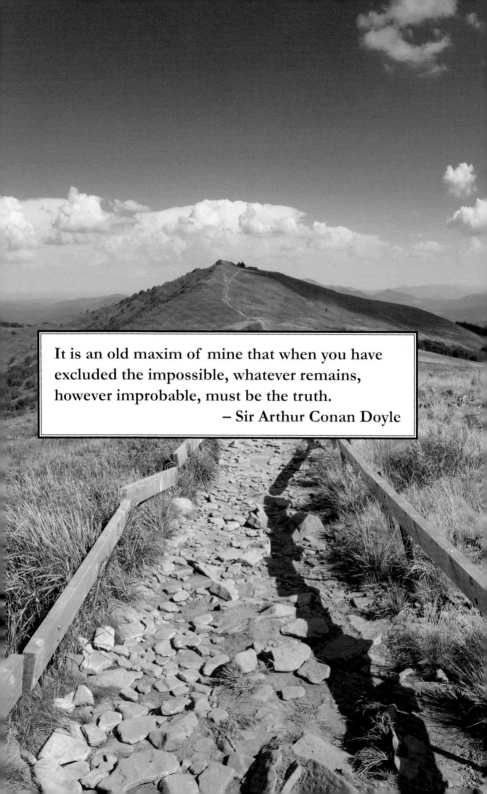

It is an old maxim of mine that when you have excluded the impossible, whatever remains, however improbable, must be the truth.

— Sir Arthur Conan Doyle

CHAPTER 11

DETECTING SIGN

Whenever a person walks through an area, whether it be at home or in the wilderness, evidence is left of that passage. A person must contact his or her environment in order to travel by foot. In fact, walking, the most common type of unaided travel, requires a person to come into contact with their environment approximately once every 18 to 20 inches. Some disturbance (sign) is made through that contact and the first phase of tracking incorporates detecting this sign. The next phase of tracking includes following a track after finding the initial sign.

TWO PHASES OF TRACKING

1. **Sign Cutting –** detecting the first sign from which to track.
2. **Tracking –** following a trail of sign.

Vision[1]

Before jumping right into what sign looks like, the acts of "looking" and "seeing" need to be addressed.

---

[1] C.E. Worsham, Techniques of Tracking on Various Ground Covers (private publication, 1989), pp. 2-3, 11.

Every day we all participate in the act of looking. We look at each other, we look at traffic signs, we look around, we look forward to going home after work, and we look funny on occasion, too. But, what do we actually see when we look? Most people in an urban environment, frankly, don't see much at all. They simply look. The sights they view are stark and consistent, usually full of color, rarely require close scrutiny, and are easily discernible from their surroundings. Let's face it, most folks in today's world are passive viewers, seeing only what they need to see to get by. In tracking, as in most natural settings, this type of vision—passive, non-aggressive, unconscious—will not work.

> **When tracking, a tracker must not only know what to look for, he or she must know how to look.**

When tracking, a tracker must not only know what to look for, he or she must also know how to look, and subsequently, "see." In a natural or wilderness setting, colors are not as stark and bold as they are in an urban environment. Nature has a way of using milder tones with uneven boundaries, rougher textures that tend to blend objects into each other, and weaker contrasts that make delineating one object from another more difficult. An unconscious, urban approach to looking will not lend to a successful tracking career. In the natural environment, what we see is not always what we are looking for. Therefore, we must adjust our viewing skills to interpret more clearly what nature has to offer, and learn to see what once we only sought.

If a tracker looks for certain signals or visual cues (cue: a stimulus that guides behavior) that catch the eye, rather than tracks or prints, then, in the end, far more will be seen. When a tracker has a preconceived notion of what he or she is looking for, much of what could be of help is disregarded. A tracker must keep an open mind and look at everything that might

> We must adjust our viewing skills to interpret more clearly what nature has to offer, and learn to see what once we only sought.

possibly be of assistance. From there, bits of information can be objectively disposed of, rather than unintentionally ignored.

Common Visual Cues

To see a track or print, a tracker first needs to be able to discern one or more of certain common visual cues. These cues not only offer a specific attraction to seek, they serve well as general categories of sign. These items are what a tracker should be seeking:

WHAT A TRACKER LOOKS FOR:

1. Outline
2. Shape
3. Contrast
4. Color
5. Texture

1. **Outline** - boundary or perimeter line around an area, delineating it from its surroundings. May be a small line or a complete track perimeter.

2. **Shape** - large enough to be human; i.e., usually involves flattening, unusual for environment.

3. **Contrast** - difference in color, texture, or shape from its surroundings. The greater the difference, the more compelling and attractive the cue.

4. **Color** - wavelength of light as seen by the eye and interpreted by the brain. Nature usually has mild tones, but differences can be detected. Not nearly as important in natural environments as in man-made ones.

5. **Texture** - rough or smooth; the consistency or smoothness of a surface.

If the tracker looks for these cues rather than just tracks or prints, much more is seen, and much more information is available to the tracker for interpretation. Don't look for the whole; look for the parts. When the parts are found, the whole can be compiled.

> **Don't look for the whole, look for the parts. When the parts are found, the whole can be compiled.**

Note that most of the visual cues described are simply different ways of saying, "look for something that does not belong." When something out of the ordinary is seen, there is a good chance that it can be valuable to a tracker. Thus, all of the cues listed are essentially different types of contrast in that they all have the tracker looking for abnormalities. (i.e., differences in shape, in color, in texture.)

The last consideration regarding vision that should be mentioned is that certain guidelines must be followed if any longevity and effectiveness is expected from trackers. To see more completely and for longer periods of time, trackers need to exercise their vision so that they do not become "numb" and regress back to looking rather than seeing.

> Anyone can track an elephant with bleeding hemorrhoids through a snow bank, and most think I can track a piss ant over a hot, granite boulder. Where I want you to be is somewhere in between.
>
> – Ab Taylor to tracking students

"Looking" Guidelines

These guidelines can help the searcher get the most out of his or her sight when it is needed:

HOW TO SEE
1. View both small objects and overall picture
2. Look for visual cues
3. Don't look for preconceived shapes or objects
4. Don't look for the whole, look for parts of the whole

1. Change views from the big, overall picture to the small objects regularly. Varying the focus can stimulate the eyes as well as the mind and help prevent unconscious, passive viewing and promote active, aggressive vision. The Point of a tracking team can quickly tire from examining small evidence intensely over long periods of time.

Looking up and away from the microenvironment can bring back perspective and allow the tracker to see what was invisible just a moment ago.

2. Look for visual cues, not for preconceived shapes or objects. Move in and inspect more closely anything that seems out of the ordinary or falls into a category of sign (i.e., outline, shape, contrast, color, texture).

3. Avoid any preconceptions and look at everything. Take your time. There will usually be a lot to see.

4. Don't look for the whole; look for parts of the whole. There are more of them and they can lead directly to a desired objective.

Fragments of prints are common in most terrain.

Sign - the Specifics

Before going into the subtle details of sign, let's consider what can be learned from one single footprint. The following is a list of some of the information available from a single print:

1. Length and width can help identify the print and distinguish it from others that may be similar. Size of a print can also give a rough idea of the person's size.

2. The general type of sole (if discernible) can help distinguish it from others as well as offer an aid in describing the print to searchers.

3. Measurements of specific parts of a sole pattern can help positively identify a print. That is, lug sizes, areas of wear, or pattern dimensions can help distinguish one print from others.

4. Several prints in a row can help determine direction of travel and stride, which can aid in finding subsequent prints.

Even though it is rare to find a complete, clear print, fragments of prints and sign will be common in most terrain. Because of this, as much information as possible must be learned from each piece of sign. Tracking is not a race to see who finishes first; it is an exercise in accuracy and efficiency. There is no excuse for losing the

> **Tracking is not a race to see who finishes first; it is an exercise in accuracy and efficiency.**

trail. Getting there quickly is worthless if you end up at the wrong place.

Drawing a print, particularly a complete and identifiable one, can help others to know what print to seek. The drawing can be copied and handed out to searchers so that one specific print can be sought, thus lessening the possibilities. When time allows, drawing a print, or a part thereof, is always a good idea. A standard track report form that offers an area to draw and describe a print is good for this purpose (see this form in the appendix).

It would be impossible to mention all the different types of sign that exist because sign varies so much with terrain, weather, time of day, vegetation, and more. Here, therefore, only the most common types of sign and their general categories will be addressed.

> **Sign varies with terrain, weather, time of day, vegetation, and more.**

Sign depends greatly on the environment in which it is produced. A marsh may produce completely different sign than would a desert, for instance, but some similarities do exist. These similarities must be understood by all trackers, but it's still important that a tracker be familiar with the sign most common to his or her region.

In addition, as mentioned earlier, sign can be conclusively human or corroborant. Conclusively human sign is a disturbance which, when considered on its own with no other evidence, can be said to have been definitely caused by a person and not an animal. Corroborant sign, on the other hand, is disturbance that is not decisively human and could have been caused by an animal. This type of sign may corroborate other evidence, but, when considered on its own, is not conclusive. It cannot be determined to have been definitely caused by a person, but it may confirm or substantiate other evidence with which it may be found. While conclusively human sign is often discovered by very unskilled trackers (jump tracking), corroborant sign is not. Frequently, corroborant sign is obvious to a skilled tracker yet invisible to the novice; and, when a novice does discover such disturbance, it is usually misinterpreted. Also, corroborant sign, which by itself proves nothing, would most certainly have been caused by the person being tracked if it were to fall exactly between

Conclusively human sign is a disturbance that can be said to have been definitely caused by a person and not an animal.

Corroborant sign is disturbance that is not decisively human and could have been caused by an animal. It cannot be determined to have been definitely caused by a person, but it may confirm or substantiate other evidence with which it may be found.

two other pieces of sign at approximately a stride's distance. Because of this, corroborant sign can be as important in the long run as conclusively human sign and should never be overlooked or ignored.

Specific sign will be described below in terms of what might attract the attention of the tracker (visual cues), its general category, and whether it can be considered conclusively human or corroborant evidence.

1. Compression/Flatness
(shape, outline, contrast)
Conclusively Human

In tracking, it has generally been accepted that only people and hoofed animals can make flat spots on the ground. However, hoofed animals tend to produce smaller disturbances which have a sharp ridge that is deeper around the edge of the print. When in doubt as to the producer of certain sign, try stepping next to the flat spot using a normal walking motion. If the disturbance you made does not resemble the flat spot in terms of depth or size, you are probably looking at animal sign. It might also be valuable to know that most flat spots are produced by humans.

Flat spots cause less shadow than their surroundings, especially in good, low-angle, light.

In North America, only people make flat spots of this size and shape.

2. Compressed Pebbles and/or Twigs
(outline, shape)
Conclusively Human

Pebbles/stones can be pressed into the ground and so can twigs.

It usually requires a hard surface, such as a shoe or hoof, in order to compress a pebble or a twig into the ground. Animal paws are soft and do not cause such a disturbance. If the ground is soft enough to allow a soft paw to depress such objects, it is also likely to be soft enough to reveal the entire paw print. Again, try stepping next to the sign yourself. If the sign you produce is similar to that which you see, you could be dealing with a piece of human sign.

3. Rear Edge of Heel
(shape, outline)
Conclusively Human

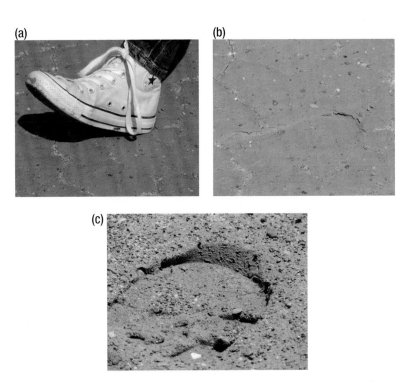

(a) The heel most often strikes with the greatest pressure and can provide the best chance to detect an impression on firm ground (b). For the same reason, the heel strike is often the deepest part of the print (c).

This is one of the most common pieces of conclusively human evidence. When a person walks on level ground, full body weight is transferred from one foot to the other by, first, contacting the ground with the rear edge of the heel and, subsequently, as the body is propelled forward, the remainder of the foot. If a disturbance will be made on the ground, this initial heel strike is when it will occur. This initial impact is when the greatest weight per square inch is applied to the ground with the sharpest part of the shoe: the rear edge of the heel.

4. Toe Digs
(outline, shape, contrast, texture)
Conclusively Human

Toe digs are often misinterpreted by novices and in soft soil can actually produce a print shorter than the footwear that made it.

This is commonly regarded as insignificant by the untrained tracker, despite its accurate indication of human passage. To propel a body forward, the rear foot pushes off in a way that either compresses the ground, moves loose material slightly backwards, or digs in. Experience makes this sign easier to interpret.

5. **Bent Low Vegetation (grass, ferns, etc.)**
   (shape, color, contrast)
   Conclusively Human

Anything that walks can push down grass or similar vegetation, thus causing the vegetation to reflect light differently. But, there are ways to differentiate human from animal sign in this type of terrain. The length

> **Hooves tend to cut vegetation because, unlike a flat sole, they may have sharp edges underneath.**

of the human foot causes more grass to be depressed than, say, a deer's. So, a longer area of flattened grass is probably human. Width, too, is relative to the beast. Animals such as cattle leave a wide pushed-down area, humans leave a foot-sized area compressed, and small game leave a narrow disturbance in grass. Hoofed animals tend to cause a crimping of grass as they push it down, whereas humans, with a longer, smoother sole, tend to simply flatten it. Look for creasing, or folding, of pliable leaves. Creasing, without hoof damage, is a good indicator that something with a flat foot passed. In dried leaves and grasses, also look for crumbling or cracking of the dead material.

(a) (b)

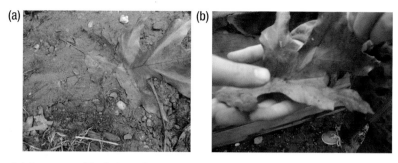

Print on ground includes a brown leaf. The edge of the shoe left a crease in the leaf (left). Same leaf, up close, showing crease (right). A crease is also easily seen in a green leaf or blade of grass.

6. Bruised Vegetation

(contrast, color)

Conclusively Human

Vegetation damaged by being stepped on heals at a predictable rate. If they are knocked over, plants may become upright within a day of being trampled, although they may bear the scars or bruises of the incident for far longer. Discolored or flattened areas on vegetation are not usually caused by small animals, and larger hoofed animals that would damage plants should most certainly cut. As with the grasses and ferns, watch for creasing.

(a) (b)

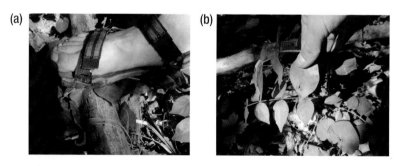

(a) Stepping on green leaves can injure plants, especially when done against something hard. This discoloration and slightly damaged area of the plant (b) is called "bruising" and heals at a predictable rate.

7. Picking Up Mud
(contrast, color, texture)
Conclusively Human

"Picking up mud," in tracking, means that mud, usually of the sticky, moist type, has adhered to the footgear. Unfortunately, as this situation continues, mud accumulates on the soles to such an extent that it completely masks any specific sole patterns that may otherwise be left on the ground. Walking with mud on the shoes like this leaves only numerous, non-distinct marks on the ground at regular intervals and, occasionally, blocks of mud that have fallen off. When the mud is of the right consistency, the chunks that fall off may hold valuable information regarding the sole pattern from the footgear that produced it.

Mud has accumulated on soles so that no distinct tread is left when walking. This can also be the source of "transfer" (see #9).

8. Shine

(contrast, color, texture)
Conclusively Human

Unlike most types of sign, shine can often be easier to see the further the observer is from it. Shine requires an oblique light and viewing angle that causes even the most subtle flattening of an area to reflect light differently. A tracker viewing from close up can overlook shine, but stepping back and viewing from a low angle or viewing far ahead can sometimes bring to notice what otherwise might be missed. This can be especially true on hard ground or when tracking through grass which tends to lay down when walked on. Close up, any sign may be difficult to distinguish, but shine becomes evident when the area is viewed from a distance. Flat ground is probably the most difficult type of terrain on which to track, but it's also perfect for seeing shine. When sign is imperceptible on flat ground at close inspection, look ahead for shine. Sometimes this may be the only way of finding anything. Because distance aids so much in seeing this type of sign, tracking by shine can be effective from aircraft as well.

Note how impacted areas reflect light differently. This "shine" may be hard to see up close.

9. Transfer

(shape, outline, contrast)
Conclusively Human

When a subject walks from one type of terrain to another, material from the first is often transferred to the second. For instance, a person walking from mud to asphalt almost always leaves some mud, often in the shape of a print, on the asphalt. As the mud falls off of the shoes, the prints diminish and eventually disappear. Usually not before, however, a direction of travel is indicated. This type of transfer can also occur when traveling from dust to pavement, from wet to dry, from fresh cut grass to pavement, from snow to pavement, or from any terrain where some material can be picked up by the footgear and deposited later. The problem lies in the fact that this type of sign is almost always short-lived and soon disappears.

Examples of transfer. (a) Transfer of snow onto pavement. This sign could be destroyed easily by the passage of one vehicle or a few minutes of sunshine. (b) Moisture and mud transferred onto large rock on which someone stepped. (c) Moisture from footfall transferred onto dry leaf. This will not remain long. (d) Mud transferred onto downed tree.

10. Displaced Twigs on Ground
(outline, shape, contrast)
Corroborant

Fallen twigs and small sticks can cause an imprint or leave an outline on the ground over time. A moving person or animal could easily travel by and move the twig from its resting place, leaving the imprint or outline behind. The direction a twig is displaced is not always an accurate indicator of the direction of travel, so don't be fooled. Keep in mind that animals can also cause this type of sign; so other evidence must be discovered in the area to corroborate the initial sign.

This twig has been moved from its "pocket" on the ground.

11. Fallen Leaves/Petals
   (contrast, color)
   Corroborant

Although leaves or petals may fall off naturally at certain times, living plants do not usually eject them without being subject to some force. They must either be pulled off intentionally, or jarred from their attachment by a substantial stress. The presence of fresh leaves or petals on the ground and next to a plant are a good indication that someone or something of fair size has passed by, hitting it. This is also true of green limbs and twigs. If the material has been trod on, watch for creasing. If the leaves or petals are dead and dried, and you suspect they have been walked on, look for crumbling and cracking of the plant material on the ground.

12. Dislodged Rocks/Pebbles
   (outline, shape, color)
   Corroborant

Pebbles and rocks behave the same as twigs in that they make a home for themselves by settling into a depression in the ground over time. Similarly, a person or an animal can disturb the objects, but this tends to need more pressure than is required for twigs. The dislodging of larger rocks from their resting places is rarely caused by animals; so the larger the rocks and the more they are displaced, the better the chance it was caused by a human. In addition, pebbles and rocks almost always tend to become dislodged in the direction of travel.

This small stone is displaced from its "pocket." This is rarely caused by animals and tends to happen in the direction of travel.

13. Broken Branches and Twigs
(shape, contrast, color)
Corroborant

A person walking on a twig, particularly a small one, will often break it. In addition to breaking the twig, hoofs usually cause splintering and an impression of the twig in the ground. On its own, splintering is not peculiar to animals. Generally, the larger the diameter of the broken branch, the more likely something the size of a human was responsible for the damage. Branches broken while still attached to their parent plant can indicate direction of travel (broken in the direction of travel); where a branch has been broken above a height of about three feet from the ground, especially a larger branch, then a taller animal, often human, is probably the cause of it. Look immediately below such sign for evidence of a hoofed animal. If none is found, it is more probable that a person was responsible. Whenever broken twigs and branches are discovered, look for other corroborating evidence that it was caused by a human.

(a)

(b)

(a) A twig broken about three feet off the ground in an area dense with small trees and bushes. Note green color, which means it is relatively fresh. As the plant heals over time, this color will change. The direction of travel is usually in the direction of the break. (b) Blackberry thorns missing from vine; green indicates they were recently removed. These vines will often be pulled, and remain intertwined, in the direction of travel.

14. Plant Leaves Close to Ground
(shape, contrast, color)
Corroborant

Broad leaf plants that grow low or close to the ground appear in almost all terrains. Very often, a person walking over or very near this type of vegetation will cause some type of disturbance. One of these possibilities is often termed "flagging" and is caused by the lighter-colored underside of one or more leaves being turned up. Generally, the more unnatural the position of the leaf or leaves, the more recently the disturbance occurred. This is because all plants tend to mend themselves over time. Exactly how long it takes for a leaf to return to its normal position differs from plant to plant; unless completely killed, they will all heal. Other disturbances to this type of plant include bruising and picking up small pebbles. Bruising is caused by a person or animal stepping on a leaf and injuring it, and is best seen on the lighter underside of the leaf. It looks like a dark green wound when fresh, eventually turning even darker, and then finally scars, turning a light brown or gray. This damage can be invisible from a standing position and often requires close scrutiny and turning over the leaf for discovery. When soft, moist leaves are compressed by something walking on them, small pebbles and particles of dirt from the ground often stick to their undersides. Brush off the clinging sand and soil and look for bruising caused by the particles being pushed into the leaf. Don't forget to look for creasing, cracking, and crumbling if the leaves are dead and dried.

(a) With the exception of the area in the center of the photo, notice how most of this ground cover is not disturbed or pressed into the ground. Closer observation (b) shows fresh bruising on the underside of some of the leaves that were compressed. (c) These low-hanging leaves were turned up as someone passed by. They currently show their lighter-colored underside, which is not their natural state. This is referred to as "flagging."

15. **Intertwined Vegetation**
    (shape, contrast)
    Corroborant

Some small bushes and grasses grow close together, and their leaves or branches overlap. When a traveler passes through an area with such plants, the limbs or leaves are often pulled in the direction of travel. Because of the close proximity of the limbs, they can catch on each other, interlace, and do not return to their natural state until they are disturbed again. Inspection of this type of vegetation can show not only that something has passed by, but also its direction of travel. The thickness of the branches and their height from the ground can suggest how big the animal or person was that caused the disturbance.

16. **Lichen and Moss**
    (shape, outline, contrast, color, texture)
    Corroborant

Lichens and mosses are soft materials that tend to yield readily when pressure is applied to them, then return to their normal states upon release. However, when either is compressed between two hard objects, such as between a shoe and a rock or tree on which the material may grow, some damage usually occurs. Like other plants, these can bruise or discolor to indicate some type of disturbance. They can also be easily damaged or displaced by the friction of a passerby. Moss or lichen can grow high above the ground on a tree or rock: when damaged, the height from the ground and the amount of disturbance may suggest a human traveler. Moss or lichen may also be the only way to get sign from rock on or near the ground. So, inspect carefully any moss or lichen on rock in the path of a traveler. Both can be sensitive indicators of a passing person.

This moss has been compressed. Is this conclusively human?

17. Dew and Frost Trails
(shape, contrast, color)
Corroborant

These trails are disturbances found where dew and frost cover an area. This type of sign is most easily discovered on manicured grass such as that found in city parks or on golf courses, but can also be found on tall grasses and grains. When a large animal or a person passes over an area that has frost or dew on it, the pressure from their feet causes the dew to disappear, the frost to melt, or an impression to be formed. In any case, the light-colored covering material (dew or frost) is removed or flattened to reveal the darker vegetation underneath. This dark-on-light contrast is easily discernible and often reveals, if discovered quickly, the exact outline of the foot which caused it (conclusively human). In essence, then, a dew or frost trail is actually a trail where dew or frost is absent.

Track in dew-covered grass. Note that it will be gone soon after the sunlight hits it, so it must be discovered quickly.

Dew and frost, depending on the ambient temperature, are caused by moist air coming into contact with cold objects, such as plants, and condensing. This condensation will remain until either it is knocked off or the ambient temperature or sunlight increases to evaporate the dew or melt the frost. The obvious trails left on short grass have been mentioned, but tall grasses, weeds, wheat, ferns and the like can also indicate disturbance by lack of dew or frost. Close inspection of vegetation early in the morning when dew and frost are most common may indicate disturbance, and is often the only type of sign available on a lush forest floor where vegetation quickly returns to its

> **Unlike most sign, grass trails may be easier to see when viewed with the light source at your back.**

normal position once trodden. A continuous line of such sign could be caused by an animal. Somewhere along the line, however, there is bound to be some other evidence that would indicate who or what has passed.

Because of the nature of this type of sign, it must be sought early in the morning. Fortunately, this is also a good time for proper light angle from the sun. Dew and frost disappear quickly in most regions, so to use them effectively a tracker must get at it early and know what to look for.

18. Excrement
   (shape, color, texture, smell)
   Conclusively Human or Corroborant

Most people are reasonably familiar with the usual consistency and amount of feces produced by humans. If questionable material is discovered while tracking and there is doubt as to it producer, be aware that human feces does not usually contain hair. However, animals that might produce similar types and amounts of droppings do contain hair. A gentle probing of any discovered fecal matter with a stick can be worth the trouble and associated nausea.

The information available from human feces when considered as sign should not be underestimated, no matter how difficult the subject is to address. Color, content, consistency, temperature, odor, and insects can all convey substantial information about the material's producer. Very black feces, for instance, can indicate a great deal of iron in the diet or a substantial intake of certain medications or chemicals. If the color is more yellow, anemia is likely to be a problem. Certain foods, such as corn, orange pulp, and some vegetable products, tend to pass through the digestive

(a) (b)

This type of evidence can tell a lot about its "supplier," and serves well as a "portable" track trap. (a) Canine scat; (b) White-tailed deer scat.

system relatively unchanged and can be seen in the feces after passing. In general, medications can turn feces most any color, depending on the chemicals involved. So knowing what the subject has been ingesting can be beneficial in identifying droppings; conversely, the droppings can help indicate what the subject has ingested. The temperature of fresh excrement is always warm, but tends to cool and dry out as time passes. Fresh feces require little weight to cause an imprint on it. The older it gets, the more pressure is required. Another fact that can be of interest to a tracker is that fresh excrement tends to draw flies (in the right season), whereas older feces (usually older than a day) will not. You may be able to catch more flies with honey than vinegar, but fresh feces can do better than both. Also, as the excrement ages, it grows a crust on its exterior and gets

> I worked in the Border Patrol with a man who seemed to make a study of human excrement. A quick observation was usually all it took for most people, but this man would probe and examine the stuff until he could tell whether the producer was a Democrat or Republican. While I admire his tenacity in extracting the maximum amount of information from this type of clue, I deplore his complete lack of common sense. Actually, I think he made such a big deal out of it because it moved slowly and he didn't have to expend much energy to study it.
>
> – Ab Taylor

darker in the sun. The older the material, the thicker the crust and the darker the sun-exposed side becomes. Rolling it over may offer some clue as to its age.

> Old men forget to zip their pants up. Real old men forget to zip them down. I won't tell you which of these apply to me, but please give me a minute while I change my pants.
>
> – Ab Taylor

The most valuable excrement to a tracker is produced by the rabbit, deer, sheep, and other animals capable of excreting small, spherical feces, which dry quickly and easily reflect the fact that they were stepped on. On the hardest ground, this type of clue may be all that is discoverable.

Urine, when discovered by a tracker, can also be helpful. Determining that urine is of human origin is a problem that would definitely require more evidence to confirm. But, after confirming that the sign is from the person being sought, the color can be useful in determining some information about that person's health. The darker the urine, for instance, the more hypohydrated the person is likely to be. The deeper the orange color of the urine, the less likely the tracker is to find the subject healthy. Urine is easiest to see in the snow, but can occasionally be discovered in other environments.

19. **Discarded Material**
(shape, color, contrast)
Conclusively Human or Corroborant

Relevant discarded materials, in reality, are not found frequently while tracking; however, if found near the trail being followed, they should certainly not be ignored. If some information is available about the person being tracked, like what he or she was carrying, or what type of gum he or she chews, then certain discarded items could be considered conclusive sign. Most of the time, litter is everywhere, and the problem lies in determining which material is relevant. A good subject profile is necessary for just this reason. This profile would tell what the subject is carrying, if possible, and what habits might produce discarded materials (chewing gum, smoking, chewing toothpicks, candy, etc.).

A Missing Person Questionnaire is a good basis on which to build a subject profile (see appendix).

Discarded material can tell a revealing story, but don't expect to see too much of it that is truly relevant.

20. Identifying Marks
(outline, shape, contrast)
Conclusively Human

Every type of individual footgear has unique characteristics that distinguish it from other similar gear. Every person is built a bit differently and, therefore, walks differently. This walk, unique to every individual, causes wear on the sole of the footgear to vary in a similar fashion. The older a shoe and the more it is worn, the more distinctive these differences in tread become. Two shoes of identical make will cause subtly different impressions on the ground depending on the wearer. When a tracker comes across a clear (complete or partial) print, he or she should make every effort to determine what distinguishes this print

What distinctive markings do you notice here? Note the significant wear on the lateral lugs and stars in the forefoot, and that the star in the heel has been cut.

from others similar to it. It may be a cut, a specific wear pattern, or something else. When you, as a tracker, find several prints of similar design, you need to know which is the one you seek.

Sometimes all that is visible on the ground are patterns that obviously do not occur naturally, such as herringbone, lines, circles, etc. These are conclusively human, but may require other evidence to determine if they belong to the person being tracked.

CLASSIFICATION OF PRINTS

Classification	Difficulty	Description
Class 1 Print	Very Easy	Perfect, complete
Class 2 Print	Easy	Complete
Class 3 Print	Moderate	ID, but partial print
Class 4 Print	Hard	Human, but no ID
Class 5 Print	Severe	Sign only

Next to creating life, the most important thing a person can do is save one.

– Abraham Lincoln

CHAPTER 12

SIGN CUTTING

Sign cutting has already been defined as the act of looking for sign in order to determine a starting point from which to begin tracking. Now, more of the details of sign cutting will be addressed by answering three questions about it: when (when is sign cutting performed), how (how is it done), and where (where is it done)?

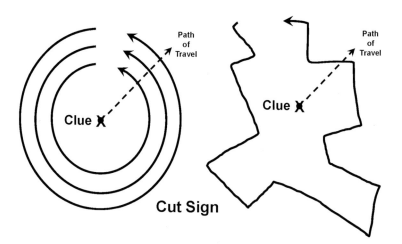

Cutting sign around a clue in order to determine direction of travel. The key is to close the loop, which does not have to be a circle. Any polygon will work (right), and the search can be expanded and repeated, if necessary (left).

When?

The best time of the day to seek track and sign is when the sun is low in the sky, usually in the morning and late afternoon. Ideally, sign cutting should be started in the morning, suspended during midday, then be resumed late in the afternoon until sunset. This is not to say that tracking is impossible during midday or at night, but simply that morning and afternoon are the best times for using the sun to your advantage. Tracking at night is quite possible, and even easy, because the light source is totally controlled by the tracker. Tracking at midday, on the other hand, can be so difficult that it is worth spending the time doing something else. Unfortunately, in SAR, we do not always have a choice.

> The best time of the day to seek track and sign is when the sun is low in the sky, usually in the morning and late afternoon.

Sign cutting is not performed just at the onset of a search. It should be employed any time that a single piece of evidence (sign, track, clothing, etc.) is found during a search. Since it is probable that the subject was near the evidence found (if the evidence is found to be relevant), sign can be cut around it to determine direction of travel.

How?

Sign cutting is performed while traveling perpendicularly to the direction of travel of the quarry. That is, attempt to intersect the path of the subject when cutting sign to avoid confusing the trail you are tracking with that of your own. Search for sign by using the available light. Look in the direction of the light source for best results, regardless of what the orientation of the light is to your body. Make the light work for you, not against you.

> **Attempt to intersect the path of the subject when cutting sign to avoid confusing the trail you are tracking with that of your own.**

The application of some simple rules can make sign cutting easier and more effective:

1. If possible, the most experienced trackers should cut sign. If a track is located, a team should continue step-by-step while the sign cutting is completed.

2. Use the available light to your greatest advantage. Face the sun, when possible, and cut at a ninety-degree angle to the direction of travel.

3. Team members should space themselves several yards apart, but should stay in visual and vocal contact. A team of 2 trackers works best.

4. Look behind you at frequent intervals, especially if the light is not optimum.

5. You may get only one chance to see a print or sign when cutting sign. Take your time and don't miss anything.

6. Do not allow unnecessary personnel in the area where sign is to be cut. Minimize the possibility of the production of confusing sign.

Sign cutting is performed quite differently than Step-by-Step tracking. Where Step-by-Step requires examination of a small area within one stride of the last track, sign cutting requires a slow, careful visual sweep within a two- or three-stride area. Be careful, though, and let your eyes set the pace, not your adrenaline-charged feet.

Where?

The first place to start looking for sign would be where it is most likely to be found. That is, look where the person being sought spent enough time to leave good evidence. Also look where the person was most likely to have walked, and where a track should be very easy to see.

> **Track Traps are likely spots for sign.**

Sign is most easily seen where the environment enhances what we seek. You may have noticed that tracks are far easier to discover and identify when they are set in moist sand or firm, moist mud. If we identify areas such as these that allow easy sign cutting, we can use them to our benefit. These, and similar areas, are termed natural or man-made "track traps."

Some examples of natural track traps are muddy areas (especially firm mud), salt flats, fields of high grass, river and creek banks, steep embankments, and dusty roads or trails. All of these specific areas will show sign readily. The following types of terrain are also considered natural track traps, but each has its own special considerations.

(a)

(a) Man-made track trap near a construction site. (b) Natural track trap on the shore of a river.

(b)

Sign cutting demands total concentration, astute observation, and depth of experience, especially when dealing with a person who does not wish to be caught. Some may even attempt to hide or disguise their tracks—imagine that! One of the most memorable attempts I recall was a Mexican who tied cow hooves to his shoes trying to resemble a cow crossing the road. Boys and girls, here is your first lesson in sign cutting: cows do not walk on two legs.

– Ab Taylor

Roads - Dusty roads can be excellent track traps, although vehicle traffic can destroy many tracks and much evidence in only a fraction of the time it took to leave them. Find out how much traffic has traveled the road in question since your quarry passed by. Do not overlook the sides of paved roads. Traffic on paved roads tends to produce a light dust that shows sign easily.

Sand - Trackers commonly make two errors when dealing with tracks in sand; both can be prevented by understanding that sand tends to make fresh tracks seem old. Gravity makes soft sand smooth over sharp edges, causing fresh prints to look old. The nature of soft sand also tends to make prints made from high-traction footgear appear older than prints made from smooth-soled shoes. This is because the effects of wind and weather will age "lumpy" tracks more quickly than smooth tracks. Just be careful when aging tracks in sand: it can be deceptive. Also, keep in mind that,

(left) Game trail through the underbrush. People tend to follow obvious game trails in the outdoors because they are easy to follow, generally clear of obstacles, and almost always lead to water. (right) Game trail with deer tracks on an old logging road.

in deep sand, track measurements can be as much as one-half inch shorter than the shoes that made them.

Game Trails - People tend to follow obvious game trails in the outdoors because they are easy to follow, generally clear of obstacles, and almost always lead to water. Pretty much the same reasons why animals use them. These trails are great to cut sign on because if a person traveled through the area, you can bet he or she used the trail. Also, the trails may be covered with animal droppings which can serve as "portable" track traps. The feces can show sign that the surrounding terrain may not.

Man Made - Some examples of man-made track traps include plowed fields, dirt roads, firebreaks, construction sites, fences, or even a small area that was cleared purposely in order to catch a good print of anyone passing (track trap). Fences may not necessarily produce terrain that is good for detecting sign, but if the fence had to be climbed over, under, or through, then plenty of sign would most certainly be produced on even the most difficult ground surfaces. If the fence itself is rusty, a scuff mark may be visible, and don't forget to look for cloth or human hair on a barbed-wire fence. Fences can also serve to direct the travel of individuals, particularly lost ones. A lost person may welcome finding anything straight to follow, and so might follow a fence line for some time.

Other - There are other features that might also affect a person's choice of route. For instance, a person may follow a pipeline or utility line in order to reach civilization. Items such as towers, lights, and beacons can attract a lost person and therefore effect their direction of travel. Mountain peaks or terrain features that are visible from far away might cause a person to follow a certain path. Any one of these "route modifiers" could be used very effectively to determine a direction of travel. When the direction was assured, sign could be cut ahead, and sometimes far ahead, to hasten the tracking process.

> No matter how long it takes, you are not making progress unless one team is on the last known track looking for the next. Without a Step-by-Step team giving direction, all other methods of locating sign are like sailing a ship without a rudder: to achieve your goal, you have to be the luckiest son-of-a-bitch in the world.
>
> – Ab Taylor

There will be times when terrain and other features do not limit travel so very much, and you are attempting to follow a marathon hiker. These are the times when the Step-by-Step approach combined with sign cutting becomes most important. Use the terrain and track traps to assist in finding sign, and always depend on the Step-by-Step Method once a track is started. The Step-by-Step trackers will serve as a compass, constantly indicating direction of travel, therefore indicating where sign should be cut.

The most important principle of sign cutting is to do it where sign is easy to see. To assure this, periodically and carefully test the route you are following by determining if you can see your own prints. If you can't, pick another area for cutting sign.

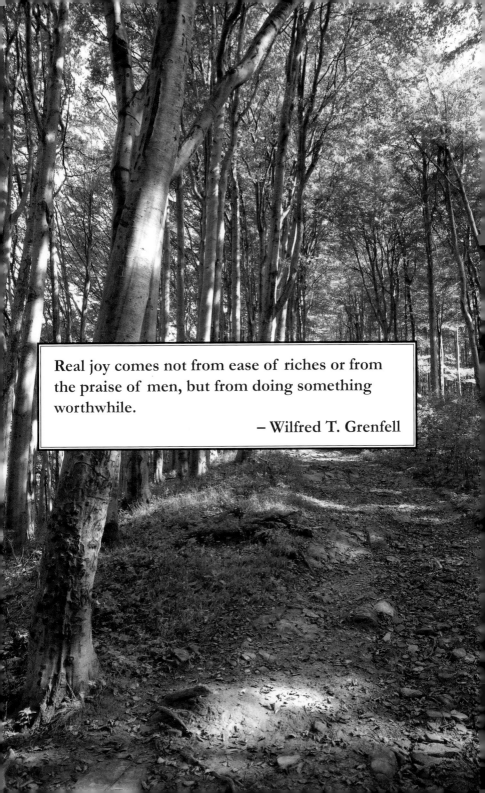

Real joy comes not from ease of riches or from the praise of men, but from doing something worthwhile.

– Wilfred T. Grenfell

CHAPTER 13

AGING SIGN AND TRACK

Knowing when a particular track or piece of sign was produced could be of great value to a tracker. Determining the age of each of several pieces of evidence, by whatever means, should help to ascertain which was produced first. It could also indicate the level of proximity to the quarry, and their direction of travel. Having the ability to age sign would remove much the guesswork from the process of placing each piece of evidence in its proper chronological order. After all, the more recently a particular piece of evidence was produced, the more distinct it will be, and the greater its value. "Time may improve wine," as an old philosopher once said; however, time does not improve the quality of sign or track left for a tracker to find.

As it does to most things on this Earth, time affects sign. An area showing track or sign tends to return to its original condition by the effect of certain forces over the passage of time. Understanding these forces can be invaluable to a tracker, but this should not be considered until a novice has grasped the fundamentals of the tracking art. Although the major forces involved in obliterating sign may be obvious even to the novice tracker, it can take years to appreciate the subtle influences at work in an environment. A novice should have an idea what forces might effect sign, but the in-depth study of aging should be considered an advanced skill that is assimilated over years of experience.

Although it is a bit beyond the scope of this text, certain concepts about aging are necessary for the novice's future education, and to make a foundation upon which experience is built. Outlining these concepts is the limit to which these topics will be discussed here.

> **Although the major forces involved in obliterating sign may be obvious even to the novice tracker, it can take years to appreciate the subtle influences at work in an environment.**

Basically, the forces of nature will affect any material or environment that can show sign. These forces can be split into two broad categories: biological and mechanical.

Biological

Biological forces are those that affect living things and are generally centered around the ability of living things to heal and/or decompose. When a living object is damaged (sign), the healing process is begun. Exactly how long this process would take to completely mask any damage is dependent on the following: the particular object (tree, leaf, bush, etc.), what type of damage was done (scratch, bruise, cut, etc.), and the extent of the damage (superficial or deep).

A tracker needs to know that this healing process exists, and that it will eventually obliterate sign.

Decomposition and decay also affect living objects and can alter sign. This type of sign degradation is usually preceded by other natural forces that act more rapidly. Nevertheless, a tracker should be aware that decay will eventually affect all living objects.

Mechanical

Mechanical forces are those which cause sign to be obliterated by the motion of objects, or by the action of forces on objects. They can be categorized into either "natural" or "man-made" forces.

The natural motion of air (wind) usually moves light objects around (sand, rain, dust, leaves, etc.), but it can also be powerful enough to move large, heavy objects. The impact on the environment of both light and heavy objects moved by wind will eventually remove any evidence of sign or track.

The natural motion of water (rain, waterfalls, rivers, etc.) can quickly destroy evidence left by a passing person. Wave action easily and quickly removes footprints from the beach, and rain can pound mud that shows a print back into flatness in short order.

Falling or blowing snow may cover old evidence and make tracking impossible. On the other hand, snow of the right consistency can make tracking a joy. When wind combines with either rain or snow, tracking can become difficult because of how quickly sign is covered or rendered unrecognizable. Snow is also affected by sun and heat. Shaded snow prints may last a long time and still appear fresh, whereas those in direct sunlight can disappear rapidly and completely.

Sun and heat themselves are natural destroyers of sign. They can affect plants by causing them to wither more rapidly, and may cause the moist soil in a fresh print to dry more quickly. A newly fallen leaf can seem to age far faster in the sun, and color changes caused by the effects of direct sunlight can cause confusion or misinterpretation.

FORCES THAT CAN DESTROY SIGN

I. **BIOLOGICAL**
   A. **Healing Process/ Growth**
   B. **Decomposition/ Decay**
II. **MECHANICAL**
   A. **Natural**
      1. **Weather**
         a. **Wind**
         b. **Rain**
         c. **Snow/Sleet**
         d. **Heat/Sun**
      2. **Animals**
         a. **Eating**
         b. **Walking**
   B. **Man-Made**
      1. **People**
      2. **Vehicles**
      3. **Other**

The motion of people and animals can act to obliterate prints as well. A good print on a heavily travelled hiking trail will usually be covered by another in a fairly short time. Animals, too, by the mere act of walking, can destroy good sign, either covering it over or rendering it unrecognizable. A good tracker should be thoroughly familiar with the area in which he or she is tracking. This will allow an understanding of how many people could have travelled over an area, how many and what kind of animals frequent the region, and when all this usually goes on. Test these variables and their impact yourself by laying prints in the area in question and returning to examine them after a set period of time (i.e., 1, 2, 4, 6, and 12 hours). Remember that it's probably better for novice trackers to either skip this exercise altogether or use the longer periods of time (i.e., 12 or 24 hrs.) for reexamination.

In terms of man-made, mechanical forces, the most common track obliterators are probably vehicles such as cars, trucks, and motorcycles. They tend to cause continuous and permanent impact damage wherever they go. Even though the areas where these vehicles travel can be great natural track traps (roads, trails, paths, etc.), their weight and motion usually destroys much of anything that could have been helpful to a tracker. In dirt areas, helicopters can also unwittingly blow sign away while attempting to help.

Humans may also have a devastating effect on tracking by moving or tampering with sign or track. What a tracker sees and interprets after such activity can be quite different from what actually occurred. At the very least, this can be misleading.

Mechanical forces can act on living objects as well. When examining for biological effects on sign, be aware that mechanical forces may also come into play and work to degrade it. Always be mindful of both biological and mechanical forces when aging sign.

Whenever the victim's sign could easily have been found and followed to a happy conclusion, some well-meaning searcher has come blissfully bumbling along unknowingly erasing every bit. I have been teaching, pleading, and begging for this ignorance to stop for the past 25 years, yet it still happens on every search I have ever been on. Not every searcher needs to be a tracker, but everyone must be track aware. As a searcher, if you are not track aware, you would do the victim's family a great service by staying home. If you still feel compelled to attend a search anyway, stay within arm's length of the command post at all times. If you can't abide by this simple rule and I catch you stepping on evidence, I will attempt to slow your progress by applying the "Texas Hobble*."

— Ab Taylor

* Editor's Note: The aforementioned "Texas Hobble" is a delicate surgical procedure invented by Mr. Taylor that involves the recipient's genitals. Suffice it to say, it's not pleasant, and we highly recommend you comply with Mr. Taylor's advice.

Summary - Aging Sign

Certain forces act upon sign and track to render it eventually unusable to the tracker. A novice must recognize these forces, as well as their potential. As the tracker gains experience, a thorough understanding of these effects must be acquired to achieve the best interpretation and use of evidence.

Learning Track Aging - The Test Bed

Leaning to age sign is one of the subtleties of tracking that comes primarily from experience. You can, however, speed up the educational process by setting up your own controlled experiments in the environment in which you will be tracking.

Find an area that accurately represents the type(s) of environment(s) in which you would be called upon to track. Lay out a series of tracks (25 or so) in a fairly straight line and mark the first and last. At preset intervals (i.e., 1, 2, 4, 6, 12, or 24 hours), return to the area and lay out a similar series parallel to the first, making sure that the first series is not damaged by subsequent tracks. Repeat this process, studying the differences in the prints and noting changes caused by the passage of time and weather. Keep a log or diary of your notes and take photos for future reference. Perform this type of testing at various times of the year, under varying weather conditions, to gain full benefit. Also, try placing the prints on game trails to see what effect specific animals might have on the tracks. Novices should start with the longer periods of time, such as 12 and 24 hours, for reexamination of the sign.

When laying out this test bed of prints, make sure to include appropriate vegetation, rocks, pebbles, sand, dirt, and any item that might come into play while you are tracking. Notice how plants heal over time, and how long it takes for the environment to return to normal. Notice the differences between fresh and aged sign and directly compare both.

Do not hesitate to take a lot of notes and photographs during the testing process; what you learn from this exercise will depend entirely on the time and energy you expend studying the results. If properly conducted, this type of testing can be invaluable to the serious tracker.

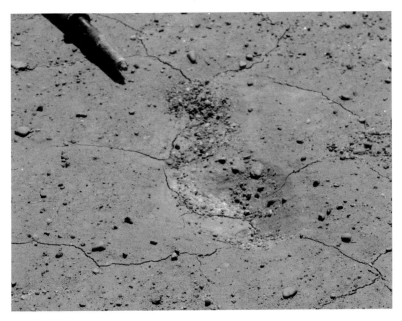

Time affects sign. An area showing track or sign tends to return to its original condition by the effect of certain forces over the passage of time. Understanding these forces can be invaluable to a tracker.

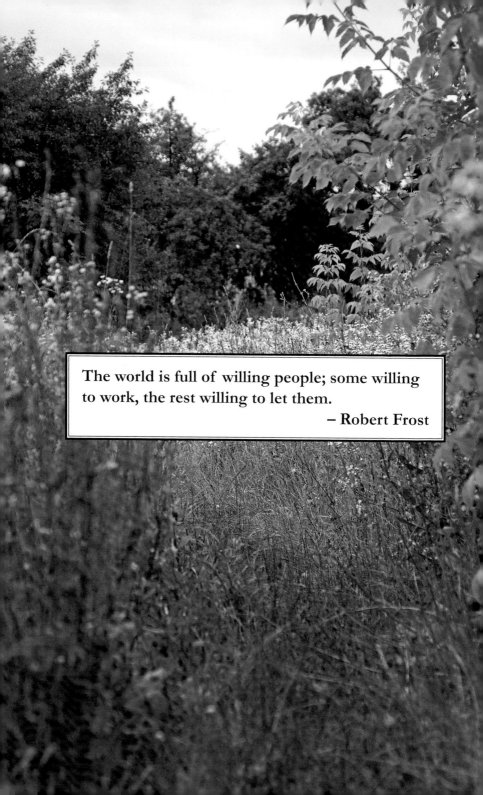

The world is full of willing people; some willing to work, the rest willing to let them.

– Robert Frost

CHAPTER 14

COMMUNICATING PRINTS – TRACK ID

It is essential for a tracker to be able to do three things with a print once it has been positively identified:

1. Communicate the track to others.

2. Differentiate the track from other similar tracks.

3. Document the description for later use.

The last two can be easily accomplished by simply studying the print, measuring it, and then drawing it. Photographing the track can be important, but much more can be learned by drawing it. Drawing the print can bring details to the attention of the tracker that otherwise might have been

> **Drawing the track can bring details to the attention of the tracker that otherwise might have been missed, and can emphasize subtle marks that might be difficult or impossible to see in a photograph.**

missed, and can emphasize subtle marks that might be difficult or impossible to see in a photograph. Photographing a track is a good idea, but should supplement, not replace, a sketch.

Study and measure every aspect of a print and indicate the measurements on the drawing. Measure, at least, the length of the track; the widest part of the sole and the heel; the length of the heel; the stride (heel to heel), if possible; widths of any lines or marks; distances between lines or marks; number and size of any geometric shapes; and the number of lugs or other sole characteristics. Be careful to note any nail holes or stitches that are evident in the print, as well as the number and sizes of any marks or lines. Search for and note any cuts, worn spots, or other details unique to the print. Everything visible should be noted and documented on the sketch. Any one of these characteristics might be what differentiates this track from others and is, therefore, important.

An interesting sole will make an interesting print.

Beware of suggesting a size for the print (i.e., size 3 or 4) from measurements made in the field. Manufacturers vary widely in their approach to sizing footgear and no standards really exist. Rather than convey an estimated size, relate the measurements (length, width, etc.). In addition, take a digital photo that includes a measuring device (ruler or tape measure) in the photo to provide scale.

The drawing and/or photo can be copied and distributed to other searchers, but occasionally the print may need to be described via radio or telephone. Tracking is almost entirely visual, whereas voice communication is entirely verbal. The skills required to perform both well are related but not the same. Practicing both is important.

When verbally communicating a track, certain ideas should be kept in mind to minimize confusion and maximize efficiency:

- Make sure to identify yourself and give your location, if necessary, as well as the direction of travel (with compass) of the track.

- Keep it simple. Paint a mental picture by using words that are familiar to everyone and to which everyone can relate. Use words that are easy to understand and whose meaning is limited.

- Begin with a general description. Is it a flat (no heel) or a heel (a distinct heel)? Continue with a term that describes the general class of footgear, if possible. (i.e., athletic shoe, sandal, work boot, hiking boot, dress shoe, cowboy boot, etc.) Beware of speculation as to the type, and know the differences before using the terms.

- As a secondary consideration, briefly describe the type of terrain and ground conditions as well as the age of the track, if you can. This might give an indication of the detail to expect.

- Give the specific details describing the sole pattern starting at one end of the print (tell which). Such details should include, but not necessarily be limited to the following:

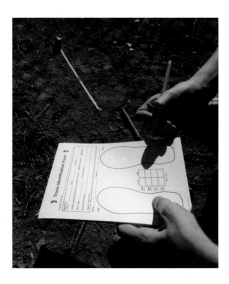

Document every conceivable measurement as well as every distinctive mark.

   a. Although all measurements should be documented, in the interest of clarity and brevity, only the length and width of the print and the length and width of the heel should be conveyed over the air. Consider using descriptive terms rather than exact measurements for radio communication. Terms like "as wide as a pencil" might be understood better than "1/4 inch."

   b. Number or type of lugs (shape, measurements, etc.).

c. Number or spacing of any nail holes and/or stitches.

d. Shape of the leading edge of the heel (i.e., straight, concave, V-shaped, etc.).

e. Shape of the toe (sharply pointed, round, square, etc.)

f. Specific shape of marks in the pattern (i.e., circle, square, diamond, oval, line, thick line, broken line, wavy line, herringbone, etc.). Avoid using ambiguous terms such as "round" and "flat," and stick to more visual terms.

Note the white "wear" mark on the lateral part of the heel of the boot on the left (a right boot). This wear indicates that the wearer walks on the outsoles of his or her feet (supination). The other boot shows similar wear, just not as much. Would these boots make a unique, identifiable print?

g. Specific way of walking. Look for dragging of feet, scuffing, toes pointing out or in, wide straddle (feet placed widely apart), consistently shorter stride with one foot, long stride (runner or jogger), or anything that may make this track unique.

h. Look for tendencies or trends in where and how the subject walks and convey them. Does the subject always walk at the side of the road? Does the subject step over logs rather than on them? Does the subject tend to walk drainages rather than ridges? Does the subject avoid brush? Does he or she walk in a straight line no matter what? If not, what tends to change the direction of travel? Fences? Wooded areas? Water?

- In sensitive situations where the details conveyed via radio are immediately important, have the receiving party confirm your description by repeating it back to you. In practice, this may be a good idea every time a print is described over the radio or phone.

- Use a standardized track report to record your findings (see the appendix).

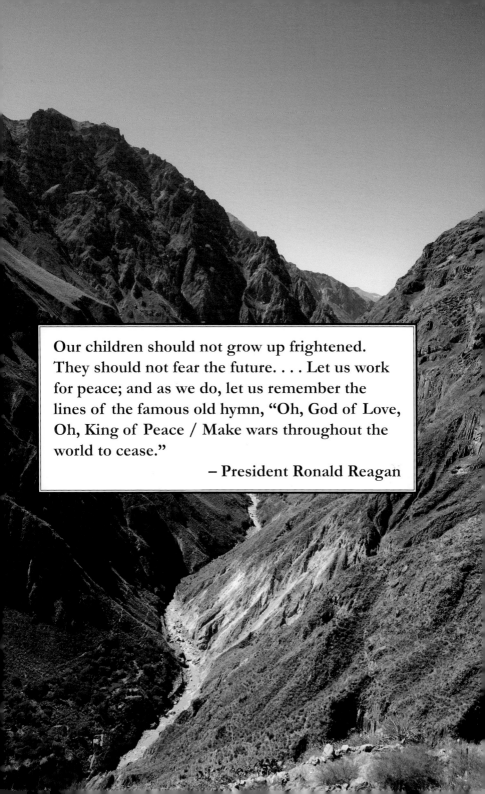

Our children should not grow up frightened. They should not fear the future. . . . Let us work for peace; and as we do, let us remember the lines of the famous old hymn, "Oh, God of Love, Oh, King of Peace / Make wars throughout the world to cease."

– President Ronald Reagan

CHAPTER 15

HANDLING EVIDENCE

Any search and rescue worker can be the first to find a lost subject or clue; established procedures should be followed to minimize problems. Whether a SAR worker finds a small clue or an injured victim, how the individual or team handles the situation may have a great effect on the outcome of the search and any potential investigation.

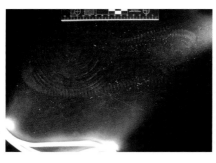

Proper processing of discovered evidence is essential. As clues are discovered, they must be recorded, interpreted and acted upon. This takes more than just the ability to track. Photo courtesy of Dana Rowsey.

Tracking can be useful in many situations, and recording the evidence effectively is an art. Photo courtesy of Dana Rowsey.

Proper processing of discovered evidence is essential for effective tracking within a SAR incident. As clues are discovered by the tracker, they must be recorded, interpreted and acted upon. This takes more than just the ability to track. It combines tracking ability with an understanding of how to handle what is discovered. If a tracker expects to catch up with the subject, clues must be handled in such a way that facilitates all search efforts, yet also preserves the evidence for subsequent investigation.

> **If a tracker expects to catch up with the subject, clues must be handled in such a way that facilitates all search efforts, yet also preserves the evidence for subsequent investigation.**

Although scene and evidence protection are not necessarily a primary responsibility of SAR personnel, a thorough knowledge of essential guidelines will serve to build better relations with all authorities, to preserve evidence, and to get the most from all clues.

Briefing

The best way to handle any clue or evidence is to have planned for its discovery and processing. The place to do this is at the briefing.

At most organized SAR incidents, before starting their assignment, SAR personnel going into the field will be briefed by a member of the incident management team. That is, information will be conveyed to the field workers concerning such things as situation status, subject information, terrain in the search area, hazards to expect, and much more. Much information will be conveyed at a proper briefing, but specific instructions regarding how to handle and act on clues can be the most important briefing information to the tracker.

Since evidence can take so many forms, instructions on how to handle it should cover all the possibilities, leaving very little to chance. Handling clues and evidence can be the single most important part of the investigation of an incident, and therefore may weigh heavily on its outcome. Trackers are often confronted with situations not common to many other field personnel. Therefore, trackers need to ask all the standard questions at a briefing while also requesting additional tracking-specific information. If this information is not provided, trackers should request answers to the following questions regarding the handling of evidence:

> **Since evidence can take so many forms, instructions on how to handle it should cover all the possibilities, leaving very little to chance.**

1. Exactly how should the evidence be recorded? Sketch? Photograph? Narrative description in writing? All of the above?

2. Exactly how, if at all, should a print or sign be protected? Cordoned off? Covered? Plaster cast? Guarded? Should someone else be called to handle this?

3. Should I act upon my interpretation of a specific piece of evidence, or should I report my findings and wait for

further instructions? To what extent can I act on what is found?

4. What should I do, as a tracker, if I am confronted with two trails? Should I act as I see fit, or report it and wait for instructions? Is splitting the tracking team up a viable alternative?

Very often, experienced tracking teams will tell the person briefing them how they will handle such situations. This may be the best course of action, especially if those charged with managing the incident are not very familiar with tracking and trackers.

The Evidence Itself

Generally, evidence can be categorized as either "physical" or "incorporeal." "Physical" evidence is something that can be touched and retrieved. Tangible objects such as shoes or gum wrappers are examples. "Incorporeal" evidence, on the other hand, is non-physical information or knowledge — intangible items that cannot be touched or held. Examples might include the subject's age, a whistle blowing, a flashing light, or a report from a witness. The effectiveness of this type of evidence ultimately depends on how well it was recorded. In fact, it is usually converted to physical evidence by field personnel. Drawings of a print, photographs of an event, and written records of what went on were once all intangibles turned into hard, presentable evidence by the tracker.

> **EVIDENCE:**
>
> - **Physical**
> - **Incorporeal**

Physical evidence is far more desirable in the long run, because it is easier to preserve for later presentation. Intangible evidence can be important, but it's just not as persuasive because its credibility rests solely on how well it was recorded. After all, which would you find more credible: a fisherman with a tale of the big one that got away, or a fisherman with a photograph of it? Physical evidence is always preferred.

Ideally, the recording and documentation of a clue and its surroundings should be of such quality that the entire scene can be re-enacted or reproduced later. The scene should be recorded so well that what went on before, during, and after the discovery of a particular piece of evidence can be accurately recounted. This can be difficult when evidence is intangible and difficult to preserve. In such cases, the recording of the event (i.e., photograph, notes, sketches, etc.) becomes the physical evidence. The better the record, the better the evidence.

The following actions taken by the tracker can help turn intangible clues into physical evidence:

1. Take notes - record the placement of clues, position of people or bodies, and pertinent facts surrounding the scene. Leave nothing to the imagination, but do not expound. Stick to the facts and be able to corroborate them, if possible. Basically, describe in prose everything that you know regarding the scene and the situation.

2. Sketch the scene - draw diagrams and pictures of pertinent objects involved at the scene and their position

DOCUMENT EVIDENCE
1. **Take notes**
2. **Sketch the scene**
3. **Take photos**
4. **Retrieve & preserve physical evidence**

relative to each other. Not everyone is an artist, but simple line drawings can be invaluable.

3. Photograph - take photographs, if possible. This is an excellent way to document a scene, but relies heavily on light and equipment availability. Be certain to include something in the photograph that will indicate scale, time, and date, if possible. Also attempt to get at least three sides (3 photographs) of any one object.

4. Retrieve and preserve - collect clues, if within the scope of the briefing. Evidence and clues should be the focus of all sketches, photographs, and documentation, but retrieving and preserving the evidence itself is the ultimate objective. Be mindful of the fact that notes, sketches and photographs may themselves become evidence.

This is a fact of life: as a tracker, you will be extremely fortunate if you ever see a LKP [last known point] that has not been totally destroyed in terms of sign. I have seen only 2 or 3 protected LKP's in 25 years. Trained searchers are getting much better, but we'll always have to contend with the "spontaneous searchers" (i.e., family and friends).

– Ab Taylor

In tracking, evidence usually takes the form of a print or sign that, of course, cannot be directly retrieved. In addition, this type of evidence is usually time-sensitive. That is, because it tends to disappear with time, the sooner this type of evidence is discovered and recorded, the more valuable it is to an investigation. Tracks, like ice cream with children, tend to disappear quickly. This means that photographs, sketches, and other documentation will usually need to be generated immediately upon discovery of such evidence. To maximize its usefulness, the tracker will need to record a print right away.

> **Evidence should not be allowed out of your possession or protection until it can be conveyed to an equally responsible person.**

Evidence should not be allowed out of your possession or protection until it can be conveyed to an equally responsible person. When evidence is considered for use in a legal case, opportunities for alteration of the evidence, by natural or man-made causes, can reduce its credibility. That is, the greater the chances that a piece of evidence could have been changed or altered, the less its significance, particularly in court. This responsibility is referred to as maintaining the "chain of evidence," and may weigh heavily on a clue's acceptability in court. To comply with chain-of-evidence rules, the evidence must always be in the custody of an identifiable person who can testify that he or she received it in a given condition from someone else or at the scene, that the item was kept safely from any possible tampering or contamination, and that the item was then delivered in the same condition to another named person. This chain is probably more important to law enforcement personnel than it is to trackers, but the need for an understanding and appreciation of its purpose should be obvious to anyone involved with what could become issues before a court.

In emergency medical treatment, an injury is treated for its worst possible condition, just to be safe. Likewise, any SAR scene where evidence is found and collected should be considered the scene of a crime until proven otherwise. This approach allows us to consider everything as evidence until we know to the contrary, thereby protecting every possibility.

Specific Situations

Four primary categories of situations may be encountered by a SAR worker. These categories have been listed in order of general severity, but not necessarily importance.

1. **Crash scene** - usually a vehicle, occasionally an aircraft, often involves injury and death, always involves important evidence.

2. **Dead body (bodies)** - may involve any number of situations that can cause harm to an individual or group. Often involves injured subjects, and always involves important clues.

3. **Injury** - same scenarios where deaths may be encountered. May involve evidence, also.

4. **Evidence** - clues are discovered and must be processed.

In any one of these situations, a SAR worker may be confronted with evidence that may be critical to the efficient resolution of a SAR situation. Usually, for a tracker, this includes sign, or evidence of a subject passing through, and thus falls into the fourth category outlined above. However, any type of evidence may be discovered, and it must all be handled properly.

Crash Scene Considerations

Crash scenes may include injury and death, but almost always involve evidence. Often the only way to find out exactly what happened is to piece together clues. How these clues are handled and processed initially may mean the difference between knowing what occurred and guessing.

At a crash scene, there are many things that responders, including trackers, can do to help victims of the incident as well as to assist the subsequent investigation. By the same token, there are actions that could hamper an investigation, further complicate the victim's situation, and even

> **At a crash scene, there are many things that responders, including trackers, can do to help victims of the incident as well as to assist the subsequent investigation.**

result in personal injury to the emergency worker. Trackers must understand their place at this type of situation.

The most common crashes in the world involve automobiles and trucks. When this type of incident occurs, local law enforcement, fire service, and emergency medical services (EMS) are often involved. One of these agencies

> **Tracking can be of value in most situations and can only enhance the effectiveness of any emergency responder.**

usually has responsibility for the scene. Since trackers may be members of any of these agencies, they should have basic knowledge of their role in a crash scenario. In a vehicle accident, tracking can be used as effectively by EMS, police, and firefighters as it can by SAR personnel. Imagine a situation where an injured passenger walks away from a serious accident, or where someone is knocked down by a hit-and-run driver. Tracking can be of value in these situations and can only enhance the effectiveness of any emergency responder.

In situations involving remote sites, SAR personnel may be asked to assist investigators in just getting to the site. In these cases, pointing out observations and subtle clues not readily apparent to the investigator could be very helpful. At sites that would be inaccessible to all but trained SAR personnel, team members could even be asked to conduct the entire on-scene investigation.

If wreckage must be disturbed to remove bodies, the county coroner or medical examiner will need to cooperate with the responsible agency. Should the investigator be unavailable, then some other agencies, authorized to do so by the coroner, can instruct the removal of bodies. Any activity concerning dead bodies must adhere to strict guidelines set down by the authority with jurisdiction over the situation.

Guidelines for handling crash scenes:

1. Proceed with caution! Safety of SAR personnel is paramount. If the smell of fuel is strong, approach from uphill and upwind.

   a. With the presence of any fuel in the area, extreme caution should be used during any activities. Absolutely NO SMOKING or use of fire- or spark-producing devices.

   b. It is imperative to assure the safety of all personnel. Do whatever is necessary to see that everyone is prudently safe; this may include leaving the scene altogether.

2. Prevent further injury to the victim or victims by stabilizing the scene. This usually involves minimizing hazards and should not be neglected.

3. Determine whether any subjects are alive or dead. If alive, begin emergency care to the best of your ability and training. If dead, secure the scene and notify a higher authority.

4. Establish a perimeter security for the site, but remember that SAR personnel, including trackers, usually have no legal authority to perform law enforcement functions and may not be able to prevent people from accessing the scene.

5. Handle any evidence such as baggage, personal effects, cargo, mail, tracks, etc. as determined in the briefing. If no such determinations have been made, protect and leave any evidence unless it is in danger of obliteration or alteration by weather or environmental hazards.

6. Document, photograph, and/or sketch all pertinent evidence, especially if investigators will rely heavily on your observations (i.e., if they cannot access the scene, or if evidence will be affected by weather or time).

Handling the Deceased at a SAR Scene

The discovery and investigation of serious injuries and accidental death can be one of the least enjoyable, but most important, aspects of SAR and law enforcement. As with most investigative cases, someone is stuck with the task of collecting clues, finding cause, and explaining a set of circumstances. The detailed study of the event and evidence of the situation is the legal responsibility of trained public officials such as coroners, medical examiners, or law enforcement officers, depending on the nature and location of the mishap. Frequently, however, evidence is produced or discovered by trackers who are obliged to help the responsible authorities as best they can.

While at times the circumstances or facts that lead up to a death may seem rather obvious, SAR workers should understand that there are certain requirements and obligations, both to the state and to family or friends. The inquiry process varies from jurisdiction to jurisdiction and from state to state, but basic guidelines that apply to SAR team members, including trackers, have been established.

The first responsibility of someone arriving on the scene is to determine if the subject is dead, alive or critically injured. If this means moving or touching the individual, then go ahead and do whatever is necessary. Proper emergency care supersedes investigation at this point, and medical treatment is never interrupted; evidence considerations take second priority. When a victim is pronounced dead by whatever rules are generally accepted, and medical treatment is deemed unnecessary, then every effort should be directed to preserve the surroundings. The same care is extended to preserve the exact position of the deceased and any associated evidence.

Observe the scene and look for clues, evidence, or indications of what might have happened. If anything in the way of tracks, imprints, scuff marks or possessions are in danger of being lost, preserve the information or the scene description by documenting it. Whichever approach to evidence handling is followed, it should coincide with the guidelines set forth in the briefing.

If close scrutiny of the area or evidence is required, the first to approach should be an experienced sign cutter who designates a "safewalk" for future travel through the area. This is done by marking the boundaries of the safewalk with tape or by simply dragging a sign cutting stick on the ground. All future entrants into the area, then, must be schooled as to how they should approach. Any sign or evidence discovered by the individual cutting sign should be immediately noted and marked (circled).

The area immediately surrounding a body or bodies should be secured with a rope, string or tape after the subject(s) is (are) determined to be dead. This physical barrier ensures not only that officials do not casually walk in and out of the area, but should also keep other curious onlookers out. Again, pay particular attention to any item within the cordoned area. In documenting whatever was observed, make sure that plenty of emphasis is placed on disturbances or movement made within the scene by SAR workers, intentional or otherwise. Failure to do this could result in being suspect of acting beyond one's authority, or even of destroying evidence. If at all possible, remain at the scene until official help arrives, even if alone. This could involve sending a passerby or another team member for help if a radio is not available. Remember the chain of evidence. Finding a clue and then abandoning it, for any length of time, could mean the difference between acceptance or refusal of certain evidence in court.

You, or someone in your team, may be required to make a written statement. This must be as accurate and detailed as possible and involve only the facts, not conjecture. Ask for advice from a knowledgeable person when considering what to include in an official statement. The counsel of an attorney may be prudent.

Unless specific instructions have been given to do so, do not search a deceased person for identification. That is an official function, and must be carried out by responsible authorities. Depending on the state and local jurisdiction, a body may only be moved or pronounced dead by a coroner, deputy coroner or medical examiner. Essentially, one of these people is in total command of the site. Often, however, SAR personnel are called upon to assist in the investigation under the specific direction of one of these officials.

Always try to have a witness to any activity you are involved with around the scene of a death. Everyone becomes suspect when the ultimate tragedy becomes reality and a human dies. Nothing is sacred and everything is possible. Most importantly: be mindful of your own interests, have a reason for all that you do, and document everything well.

Handling Injuries at a SAR Scene

Considerations for handling injuries are similar to those for handling deaths. Protecting evidence is important, but falls second to proper emergency care. Treatment of injuries and alleviation of pain is a major goal in each emergency response, and should not be precluded by the collection of evidence. However, when the treatment is complete, the entire investigation will still hinge on any clues, observations, and recollections of those involved. Therefore, be mindful of such considerations while treating a victim in any situation, and try to protect evidence while doing your best for the patient.

> **Most importantly: be mindful of your own interests, have a reason for all that you do, and document everything well.**

Summary - Handling Evidence

To summarize, handle any clue as if it were the only piece of evidence, consider each and every discovery to be absolutely important until proven otherwise, and follow these simple guidelines:

1. Plan for the handling of evidence, including tracking-specific considerations, in the briefing. Do not wait until something is found.

2. Generate an accurate record of the evidence and its environment by taking notes, making sketches, photographing, or retrieving the evidence.

3. Understand and maintain the chain of evidence.

4. Treat injuries or assist the injured first, but be mindful of any evidence, including sign.

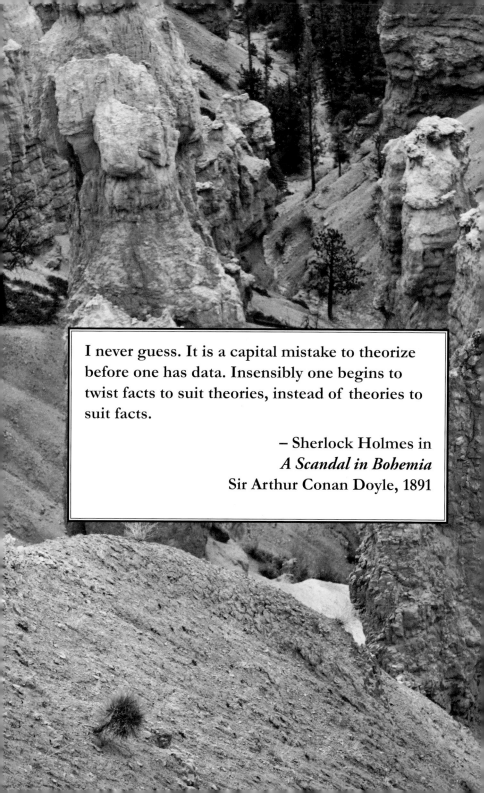

I never guess. It is a capital mistake to theorize before one has data. Insensibly one begins to twist facts to suit theories, instead of theories to suit facts.

– Sherlock Holmes in
A Scandal in Bohemia
Sir Arthur Conan Doyle, 1891

CHAPTER 16

STRATEGY

Occasionally, the tracking team is charged with organization and control of a search effort, but the proper approach is to have individuals charged with managing the situation within a function-based hierarchy. If a SAR incident is managed properly, trackers will be called to participate early in the plan. Trackers need to know their place within the structured hierarchy and to whom they answer. These topics, as well as others that are important to the tracker, are covered in any of the fine educational programs dealing with search management. Only the considerations of approach and strategy that facilitate a tracking team's specific tasks will be discussed within this text.

> **If a SAR incident is managed properly, trackers will be called to participate early in the plan.**

Initially, after dealing with any administrative details, a tracking team called to a SAR incident should attempt to determine where the lost subject was last seen or known to have been. This information may be conveyed through the command structure, or it may have to be determined by the trackers themselves. Where was the person last seen? Where did they pass or what did they do? The area where the victim was last known to have been has the highest chance of containing tracks or other evidence which can be used by a tracker to determine a direction of travel. It takes only three prints to determine direction of travel, and if you can accomplish just this much, you will have contributed more to the search than most could ever hope.

From a subject profile, a tracker should be able to guess what size print is being sought (small child, small adult, large adult, etc.) and the approximate length of the stride. If you're real lucky, the profile could offer a specific, complete print. When you have an idea what is being sought, and once an area is identified as "hot" for sign, other people should be kept away to avoid confusion or destruction of the evidence. This cannot be overemphasized. Next, cut sign around the area (perimeter cut), trying to determine a direction of travel, and note any specific additional evidence such as a complete print. Better yet, carefully approach the last known point and examine the entire area without moving around unnecessarily. If a scuff, track, or other sign is visible, stand behind it and scrutinize the area in front of it for additional evidence that might suggest a general direction of travel. Look beneath your own feet to see how they impact the area and look for this specific type of sign. Once the direction of travel has been determined from the last known point, another tracking team could cut an intersecting line. Be extremely careful not to damage any existing sign. This may be all anyone has to go on. Take every precaution necessary to preserve any prints found, then see that they are documented and communicated to others involved in the search.

> Thirty to forty minutes spent at the last known point cutting sign may be the best time investment of the search, even if you are only working a few bits of sign. Keep in mind that if you can find as few as three tracks and a pretty good ID, you will have contributed more to the search effort than 100 other searchers who are running around hoping to get lucky.
>
> – Ab Taylor

Once a direction of travel is determined, one tracking team always stays on the trail, following it step-by-step. That is, never going past the last conclusive sign. This will mean that there is always someone on the trail. Other strategies can be applied to speed up the process, some of which will be discussed; but, the importance of keeping someone on the last track can not be overemphasized.

> Once a direction of travel is determined, one tracking team always stays on the trail, following it "step-by-step."

The most time-consuming project will usually be finding the first track. This is why it is important at the onset to keep everyone (non-trackers) away until sign can be cut and certain basic information gathered (print specifics, will tracking work, etc.). It is important to be able to find a track and be reasonably sure that it belongs to the lost subject. Accuracy is more important here than speed. Once the track is positively identified and a direction of travel is determined, then the pace can pick up quite a bit in most situations.

If following the trail from the last known point is not possible, another method of speeding up the pace is to employ "perimeter cutting" (similar to sign cutting, in chapter 12). When initially cutting sign in an area, or when tracking becomes particularly slow, trackers can cut sign in a perimeter around an area where there is a good chance the subject has been. The purpose of such an effort is simply to discover sign at a farther distance from the last sign. If this perimeter team can positively identify the track and direction of travel, they can become the step-by-step team and allow the rear team to perimeter cut around them. The perimeter cut can range from several yards to several miles, depending on the terrain and how long the victim has been missing.

The shape of the perimeter can be square, triangular, circular, or any shape. It can even follow compass headings. The only requirement is that, no matter which shape is chosen, the loop must be completed. Two trackers can cut sign in opposite directions, meeting to close the perimeter, or one team can cut sign continuously until they reach their starting point again. The only exception to this rule would be when sign is found and urgency is very high but resources are limited. If no sign is found, consideration should be given to the fact that no one has entered the area.

If careful thought is put into where to cut a perimeter, much time and energy can be saved. Use natural barriers such as cliffs, large rivers, and thick brush, where a person would

> **If careful thought is put into where to cut a perimeter, much time and energy can be saved.**

not likely pass, to limit the perimeter. Use areas where track and sign is easily seen to complete the perimeter (i.e., river banks, dry stream beds, plowed fields, tall grass, steep banks, trails, road edges, etc.). Pick areas that would allow you to be certain if someone passed. Now the entire perimeter will be either easy to cut or impossible to pass through.

The same rules that apply for sign cutting apply for perimeter cutting with the following additions:

1. Do not allow anyone to walk or drive within the perimeter being cut, with the possible exception of the trackers on step-by-step who must stay with the track they are working. The most common destroyer of sign and track is people, on foot or in a vehicle.

2. Each successive perimeter cut should be made just as carefully as the first.

If a perimeter cut is unsuccessful, it can mean that the cutting team missed something or that the subject has been passed and is between the two teams. In either case, it is extremely important that once a team gets on a track, they stay there until another positive ID is made. Close is not good enough. Someone must always be on the last track after a positive ID has been made.

Vehicles are "universal track destroyers." But, because tracks are laid down in layers, vehicle tracks can be helpful in determining when a track was laid. Which came first, the vehicle or the person who made the print? Find out when the vehicle drove past and you can narrow down when the track was laid.

To improve the "quality of service" trackers can offer when involved in a search effort, it is worth referring to the following guidelines. After all, it is far better to learn from mistakes of others than from your own!

1. Get the most recent copy of the best map available for your area. A USGS 7.5 Minute Topographical map is best for foot travel. But maps can now be printed as needed in almost any scale.

2. Make sure that both vehicular and foot traffic is kept to a minimum for the best sign cutting results within the high probability area(s).

3. Check for sign and track along trails and roads on the approach to the search area. Be track aware.

4. Get as much information as possible about the lost subject(s) before going into the field. Try to obtain a detailed subject profile.

5. Only one or two of the most experienced trackers should investigate the area (cut sign) initially. This minimizes conflicting sign.

6. Preserve evidence found at all cost. Document and catalog all likely tracks and sign while traveling into the search area, and be particularly aware of tracks that travel in unusual or erratic patterns. Establish a system for sorting and discarding prints, and make sure the tracking team's prints can be easily distinguished from any others. One way to accomplish this is to put an identifying mark on the footgear of every member of the tracking team.

7. Since hazards in an area are likely spots to find the subject, they are also good areas to look for sign: look first in caves, mines, near cliffs, in holes, in ponds, etc. within the search area.

8. Make sure that a perimeter has been established beyond which a person could not pass without being noticed. In search management lingo, this is known as "confinement."

9. Cut the perimeter within the confined area, but beware of presuming that no sign on a perimeter cut means that a sector can be ruled out. The subject may have traveled into the sector after the cut.

10. Talk to everyone confronted while traveling within the search area. Presume that everyone is suspect (e.g., the missing person) until proven otherwise.

11. Look for clues, not the lost subject, but do call out the subject's name at regular intervals, and then listen for a response. Bear in mind that, depending on the individual and the situation, some people may not answer. Children as well as escaped felons tend to act alike, in that they both seem to hide when their name is called.

12. Use the Step-by-Step Method of tracking.

It is better to light a candle than to curse the darkness.

– Motto of "The Christophers"
www.christophers.org

CHAPTER 17

TRACKING THE EVADER

As you can imagine, all those whom a tracker might trail don't always wish to be found. Runaways, escaped convicts, and fleeing criminals are examples of some of the many types of individuals who may wish to remain "lost." For a tracker, following a person who does not want to be found can be challenging, at the very least. Nevertheless, almost every tracker will get a chance to participate in this adult version of hide-and-seek.

EXAMPLES OF INDIVIDUALS WHO MAY WISH TO STAY "LOST":

1. Runaways
2. Criminals
3. Escaped convicts
4. People who simply want to be alone
5. Terrorists

In this book, people who do not want to be followed or found by a tracker will be referred to as "evaders." The extent to which each individual evader desires to avoid contact varies from a seven-year-old who does not want to be spanked to a militant, terrorist guerrilla who kills without hesitation. Since virtually every subject could be an evader, it is up to the tracker to assess the level of evasion skill his or her quarry may possess, as well as the level of security risk tracking such a person might impart on the trackers. Ultimately, these decisions may mean the difference between a happy reunion and a violent tragedy.

Children are, by far, the most common evader in SAR situations. Not only do children fear their parent's wrath, but time after time, searchers are out-maneuvered by children who are simply practicing what adults have been teaching for years: stay away from strangers. Although this "stranger danger" attitude has undoubtedly saved many children from abuse, it has also been known to cause lost children to hide from rescuers. Also, consider what the child sees when approached by a search and rescue team: a group of yelling adults wearing packs, headlamps, and funny helmets, wielding sticks and whistles. They look like men from Mars. When you add four-wheel drive vehicles, horses, dogs and blaring radios, it's no wonder that children are afraid. A solution to this dilemma is not easily achieved, but the fact that children may hide from their rescuers must be understood. Trackers must understand that children, especially those under the age of ten, may be unwitting, yet very skillful, evaders.

SECURITY AND EVADER ASSESSMENT CONSIDERATIONS

1. **What level of evasion skill are trackers dealing with?**
2. **What risk (potential or real) does the evader pose to trackers?**

A program trying to overcome these types of children's fears is being taught at the elementary school level. It's called "Hug-a-Tree and Survive." "Hug-a-Tree," a program for children that teaches simple wilderness survival techniques, teaches kids that, "...searchers are your friends and they will know your name. Don't be afraid when your friends come looking for you." Visit the web site of the National Association for Search and Rescue (NASAR) for more information about Hug-a-Tree (www.nasar.org).

Lucky for us, most evaders will not take the time, nor do they know how, to conceal sign effectively or efficiently. For the few exceptions to this rule, trackers can be most efficiently utilized by confining or surrounding the area. Usually numbers are on our side.

All search and rescue personnel, including trackers, must also be mindful of the fact that most adults are allowed to become lost if they like. Many adults even look forward to such experiences and often pay a substantial premium to "get away from it all." Therefore, examine closely any evidence relating to urgency and need before rushing off into the wilds to save potential victims from themselves. This evidence might not only indicate if a search is called for; it might also suggest if dealings with an evader are probable. When there is an indication that an adult will evade searchers and this is coupled with a low urgency and need, serious consideration should be given to discounting active search techniques altogether. That is, if someone does not want to be found and might even avoid being found, and there is no serious evidence indicating that the situation is urgent, why search? You might end up tracking a vacationer who simply wanted to be left alone.

The point here is not to imply that every subject will evade searchers. Rather, it is to highlight the possibility that some people trackers are called on to track may not want to be followed or found. When evidence to that effect is discovered, it could substantially change the approach to a search, especially from the tracker's point of view.

Categorizing the Evader

The tracker has no control over how easily an evader is to track, but he or she can make qualified judgments about how skilled his or her quarry may be. Simply put, certain people are better at it than others. Some may have received training in the military; some may be quite experienced, but untrained; and others may be simply guessing at what will work. Whatever the level of expertise, the tracker must

> The tracker must determine early on in the effort how much evading skill he or she is up against.

determine early on in the effort how much skill he or she is up against. The place to acquire such information is the subject profile, which is compiled throughout the investigation.

Untrained evaders are relatively easy to deal with. Most standard tracking techniques (i.e., track traps, step-by-step, sign cutting, etc.) work because the subject is usually unaware of what is being done to catch

> The "bottom line" is: the more a subject knows about the skills being used to find him or her, the better they will be able to evade.

them. It gets difficult, however, when the quarry is uniquely aware of tracking techniques, and knows how to avoid being followed. The "bottom line" is: the more a subject knows about the skills being used to find him or her, the better they will be able to evade. A tracker needs to learn this type of information (evasion skill level) about a subject early so that appropriate measures can be taken to achieve success.

One method of measuring the evasion ability of a subject is to apply a grading schedule to each individual that categorizes them in a consistent fashion.

GRADES OF EVADERS

Grade A - Good Evader
Grade B - Fair Evader
Grade C - Poor Evader

GRADE A – HIGHLY SKILLED EVADER

a. Usually military trained, and may have a great deal of experience at evasion.

b. May be a good tracker and usually possesses exceptional outdoor skills.

c. Usually leaves little evidence of passing (i.e., covers fires well, uses stove rather than fire, tends to walk on hard surfaces, does not litter, does not need to make contact with people, good forager, etc.).

GRADE B - FAIR LEVEL OF EVASION SKILLS

a. May have some military training, but not recently or not much.

b. May have some experience at avoiding followers (i.e., basic tracking classes), but may not be aware of many tracking techniques. Some unique approaches to tracking may work, but the simplest techniques might be anticipated. Fair at outdoor skills.

c. Usually leaves some evidence of passing (i.e., may leave fire circles, may leave some litter, may walk on cuttable terrain, may make contact with people, may need to buy certain items, etc.).

GRADE C - LOW LEVEL OF EVASION SKILLS

a. Probably no military training and relatively uninitiated in tracking skills and search techniques.

b. Most standard approaches to tracking will probably work. Ill or injured individuals usually fall into this category. Little, if any, outdoor skills.

c. Usually leaves evidence of passing (i.e., litter, fire circles or pits, large amounts of burned wood, walks in track trap areas, propensity for human contact, would have to buy food to survive over long term, etc.). Hiding children usually fall into this category.

If a subject is categorized appropriately at the onset of the application of tracking resources, certain approaches to tracking may be immediately disregarded while others are quickly initiated, saving a lot of time and energy.

Factors that Affect a Successful Evasion

To understand how a subject may evade an effort to be tracked, a tracker must understand how a skilled evader thinks. Furthermore, to decide how well and how long an individual might consciously be able to avoid capture, the tracker must understand the factors that affect the ability of an evader to evade.

> To understand how a subject may evade an effort to be tracked, a tracker must understand how a skilled evader thinks.

PREPARATION

The most successful evasion situations will involve individuals who are prepared to do what it takes to keep from getting caught. A healthy, strong, well-thinking individual will definitely have the best chance, but this is rare where tracking is required in most SAR situations.

Lost people are rarely pictures of health. They often have physical and mental problems that may or may not have contributed to their situation. Evaders as a group are, therefore, healthier than most lost people. Evaders have usually made a conscious effort to get into the position they are in and therefore are a bit more prepared, at least physically, than the average lost person (if there is such a one). The success of an individual's evasion will be dependent on their physical ability to continue their quest, their mental ability to solve problems that arise, and their mental capacity to handle the stress of the situation. Basically, the better they are at surviving, by any means, the better they will be at evasion.

OPPORTUNITY

The best evaders will take advantage of every opportunity to improve their status and situation. If weather worsens, they might take a chance and travel when otherwise they would not. They might move under cover of darkness at night, knowing that most searchers are in bed, and walk in mud during a rainstorm, knowing that any tracks will be obliterated.

> **The best evaders will take advantage of every opportunity to improve their status and situation.**

Successful evaders are true opportunists. They must use everything at their disposal to meet their objective. Nothing is too sacred; nothing is too dear. Everything is fair game when their freedom is at stake.

MOTIVATION

The motivation of the evader can tell a tale in itself. If a tracker can find out what motivates the evader, he or she will have a much better idea of what they are capable. More than the simple motivation, an understanding of the depth of commitment is important to realize to what lengths the evader will go to reach their goal. Basically, the more motivated the evader, the better their chances of success.

> The cleverest and most skilled evader I have ever been cursed with tracking was a mentally challenged, epileptic, 10 year old boy. In rough, brushy, canyon country, this talented young man managed to evade some of my best Border Patrol trackers for over 12 hours in spite of the fact that he was supposed to require medication every three hours. He purposely left no identifiable prints as he leapt from behind one giant boulder to another until we finally were able to trap him against a 200-foot cliff. With no place to go, he stood up smiling and said, "You got me!" This is the same kid we expected to find seizing on the ground somewhere. Don't always believe what you hear.
>
> – Ab Taylor

Motivation is often best achieved through fear. Fear of suffering, illness, disease, pain and death top the list; but fear of humiliation, degradation, or the unknown have also been known to fuel the fires of misfortune and tragedy. If an evader is motivated by freedom, say, as would be an escaped convict, then the tracker must search further to learn why the escapee is so interested in that goal which, in this case, is freedom. Are they serving a death sentence for mass murder and have they escaped to keep from getting executed, or are they simply taking an opportunity that has presented itself? This is not to say that any escaped criminal may not be willing to do what it takes to remain free. However, most will be unwilling to perform crimes, particularly violent ones, that are far more serious than their original offenses.

If the evader has no reasonable alternatives, on the other hand, violence can and should be expected.

Motivation, commitment, and alternatives are essential considerations, because the level of security that a tracking team will require may be directly proportional to the importance the evader places on these ideas.

Principles of Evasion

The most successful evaders will follow certain guidelines, and adhere to standard principles of evasion. An understanding of these can help the tracker determine which tracking skills might be effective, and which might not.

> An understanding of the principles of evasion can help the tracker determine which tracking skills might be effective, and which might not.

The following are some of these basic principles:

1. Use everything you know. Recall past experiences and training, and remember what you learned.

2. Have a plan, but let it be flexible. Have several backup plans: don't be afraid to use them.

3. Observe and listen. Know where your followers are, and avoid them.

4. Travel only when you must, and travel when it would be least expected (i.e., bad weather, night, etc.). You are far more apt to be caught while traveling. Select times, routes, and methods of travel to avoid detection.

5. Avoid lines of communication. Stay away from roads, waterways, rivers, power lines, railroads, etc.

6. Sanitize or remove all evidence of presence and direction of travel. Leave as few tracks as possible and cover the ones you do leave.

7. Hide only after traveling as far as possible from where you are expected to be.

8. Inhabited areas should be bypassed rather than penetrated, even if it means miles of additional travel.

9. Do not follow the easiest and shortest routes. Avoid roads, trails, and populated areas.

10. Employ simple evasion techniques:

   a. Scout an area before traveling through or near.

   b. Patrol an area and learn what happens there before making any decisions regarding it.

   c. Use camouflage and be difficult to see.

   d. Conceal your whereabouts at all times.

11. Use the BLISS approach to concealment:

   a. Blend in with your surroundings.

   b. Low silhouette - stay out of view.

   c. Irregular shape - blend in rather than contrast with the environment.

   d. Small - make yourself small.

   e. Secluded location - pick a spot out of the way.

12. Travel and hide in places least likely to be searched.

13. Stay away from prominent landmarks.

14. Stay off peaks and ridges, but stay on slopes; near high points but below the ridge.

15. Take different approaches to frequented areas to prevent forming a path or trail.

16. Conceal fires or don't use them at all.

17. Avoid desert, snow and ice environments. They are the hardest to remain concealed in.

> Six convicts escaped from an Arkansas prison and were resting in the woods after being pursued by hounds and prison guards. Four of the exhausted prisoners were apprehended in a grove of trees. The two who escaped were hiding high in the trees and one tied himself in with his belt so he wouldn't fall out. The dogs probably knew this, but the guards had four prisoners after a long, difficult chase and they just didn't see the other two. Apparently, no one looked up! These same two prisoners later shot and killed a North Carolina State Trooper. Trackers using the Step-by-Step Method were eventually very useful in catching up to, and apprehending, these SOBs.
>
> – Ab Taylor

Approach to Tracking Evaders

The best approach, when it comes to tracking someone who does not want to be followed, is often no different from standard tracking techniques which involve sign cutting, clue consciousness, and the Step-by-Step Method. One difference that cannot be overlooked, however, is the need for security of the tracking team in case the evader resorts to violence to solve his or her problem.

> **The best approach, when it comes to tracking someone who does not want to be followed, is often no different from standard tracking techniques which involve sign cutting, clue consciousness, and the Step-by-Step Method.**

Depending on the risks involved, the category of the evader, and the background of the trackers, two or more security guards, called a "security over watch," may be required to offer a safe environment in which the trackers can work. These guards, whether they be military or law enforcement, travel with the trackers, keeping an eye out for anything that may impede the progress of the team. Anything from sniper fire to trip wires is possible, and the tracking team may be too caught up in their tracking to be cognizant of threats to their safety. Luckily, the Step-by-Step Method of tracking lends itself well to the concept of protection. When their lives depends on it, flankers will often ignore sign and concentrate on what's ahead, leaving the tracking to the Point. Law enforcement and military personnel recommend that a team tracking an armed and dangerous evader should be armed themselves with at least a shotgun, an automatic rifle, and sidearms. In several areas, trackers on the trail of felons are backed up (fifteen feet behind) by a special weapons and tactics (SWAT) team. Well-armed felons have surrendered without a fight when confronted with such a show of force.

A "formation" is the formal arrangement of individuals within a group and, although many formations are possible, a configuration termed the "squad line" is recommended when a tracking team requires a security over watch. A squad line allows the tracking team to work in the usual Flanker-Point-Flanker configuration, while one guard secures the group to the right and another guard secures to the left. The guards should be no closer than ten feet, but may be as far as fifty feet from the trackers, depending on the terrain; they should turn completely around on occasion to help secure the rear. This wide-line approach is less likely to surprise a subject than, say, a single file line, and allows for security with fewer chances of evidence destruction.

Another option is the "still watch" or "look out." The still watch seeks a high point from which a large area to be covered by the trackers is visible. It's important that the individual involved approaches their chosen site quietly so as not to attract attention. Then they should remain hidden, for hours if necessary, and be constantly alert for movement in the area. Night vision equipment is helpful in the dark.

Near the Mexican border, we had popular crossing spots used frequently by guides who made a living by delivering illegal aliens to rendezvous points in the U.S. These guides got quite good at figuring out how we caught them and often compensated for our methods. We frequently used dusted-off ground (track traps) to indicate when they passed, but the guides quickly caught on and began to clear off the areas after their passage. This worked until I started leaving one of my prints on the cleared areas. When I checked the areas and found my print cleaned away, I new that another "smart" guide was on his way.

– Ab Taylor

Beyond the security over watch or lookout, tracking an individual who does not want to be followed differs further from tracking a lost subject, because the evader may try to cover up his or her tracks. For an experienced tracker, this is not usually a problem because attempting to cover tracks will most likely leave more evidence. But, for novice trackers, and if considerable time has elapsed, attempts to cover tracks can end up being quite successful.

The U.S. Border Patrol enjoys a degree of success using an approach that allows the Step-by-Step tracking team to flush evaders into areas of easy egress. At a convenient and appropriate point, an ambush is set up and the evaders are apprehended as they pass. This approach is particularly effective when personnel are limited.

The key here is to get good trackers on the trail quickly so that the evidence produced by the attempted camouflaging of tracks is easier to detect. If the evader is really good (Grade A), he or she will know the trackers' art and will use its intricacies against its practitioners. These are the most difficult situations for trackers and require some skill to overcome. However, the best approach, as in all tracking, is to utilize the best trackers available, in the hope that they might see things and detect evidence that other, less skilled, individuals, including evaders, might overlook.

> **The key here is to get good trackers on the trail quickly so that the evidence produced by the attempted camouflaging of tracks is easier to detect.**

Be aware that most evaders are not Grade A, and most believe they know far more than they actually do. Because of this, they make mistakes that the tracker can use to his or her advantage. Below are some examples of what a tracker can look for when tracking an evader:

> **Be aware that most evaders believe they know more than they actually do.**

1. Look for evidence of covering of tracks such as drag marks on the ground, broken or cut branches (to scratch out tracks), long strides made by jumping, toe strikes that indicate walking backwards (while scratching out tracks), walking in streams (imprints in the silt or around the water's edge), etc. Brush marks may also indicate direction of travel.

2. Look for evidence of camouflage attempts, such as scratches with fingers in mud, broken or cut branches, torn clothing, etc.

3. Be aware of sign left by an individual crawling on the hands and knees (high crawl) or with the torso close to the ground (low crawl).

4. Evidence of running, such such as long strides with substantial impact; heavy impact around medium-sized rocks and logs (jumping over); toe-only partial prints (sprinting), etc. Look for heel drag instead of toe digs. People walking backward tend to have a shorter, more wobbly stride.

5. Examine areas for sign that might hide a road crossing (tree shadows), or a river entry (foliage hanging into water), rocks, hard areas.

6. Don't be afraid to examine possible-but-not-probable areas, especially if they are good for cutting sign.

7. Check for sign behind trees and in brush that might make a good hiding spot.

8. Put yourself in the evader's shoes. Examine what they know and their experience; consider their motivation and objective; then determine how you would do it, if it were you.

> **Put yourself in the evader's shoes. Determine how you would do it, if it were you.**

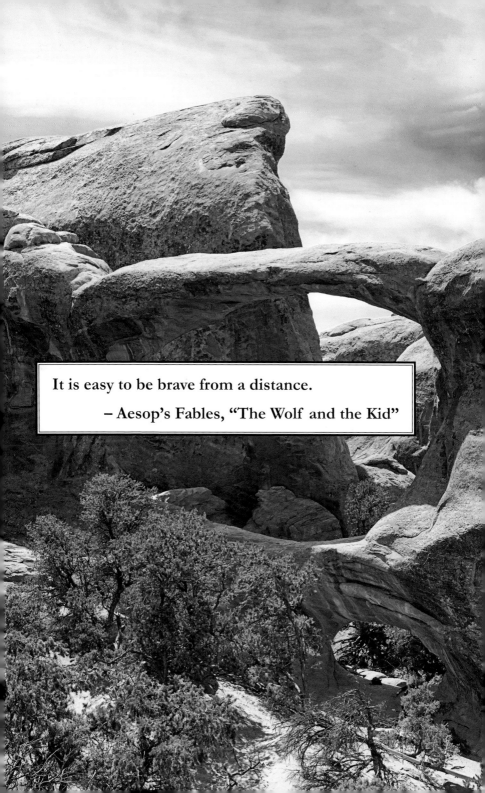

It is easy to be brave from a distance.

– Aesop's Fables, "The Wolf and the Kid"

CHAPTER 18

FURTHER CONSIDERATIONS

Now that we have reduced tracking to simple terms, it is time for an injection of reality. Tracking, although constructed of simple components, can involve some of the most complex issues in life. It deals with mysteries, grief, death, love, loss, and so much more. No dealings with such emotion-wrought topics could possibly be simple. Tracking works because it is a logical, analytical process that deals only with facts, not conjecture, hearsay or emotion.

> Looks like a prayer meeting or a crap game...
> grown people crawling around on their knees!
> Why don't they do something besides look at the ground?
>
> – Father of lost child, watching trackers

When a tracker is confronted with influences that do not contribute to the factual, logical input required, then confusion occurs. Tracking is not gaged by miles per hour, so when a tracker is rushed, effectiveness suffers. Tracking is very "sense-intensive," so when a tracker is overwhelmed with sounds, sights, and unrelated thoughts, effectiveness suffers. As a tracker, try to concentrate on what you can control. Deal with the facts. Deal with them logically, and take your time.

Where tracking is required during an incident, situations will arise that have not been broached in this text. Incident Commanders will not call out trackers because they believe, many times without a working knowledge of tracking, that tracking "…will not work here." Good trackers will not be able to get to the subject in time to find them alive. External influences will apply undue pressure, most without an understanding of the trackers art. Lost subjects may not be found. Clues may be misinterpreted. Lives may be lost.

> **Tracking works because it is a logical, analytical process that deals only with facts, not conjecture, hearsay or emotion.**

Before you become totally disillusioned, however, take comfort in this fact: the same things occur in searches every day where tracking is not employed. Lives are lost and problems arise even when tracking plays no part. Tracking is only a tool that can be used to reach an objective. It is not a panacea. But it may offer an effective option when used properly. Without tracking and its associated skills, are we really doing all we can as search and rescue personnel? Are we missing something? Could we do better?

Tracking offers another tool to apply to an age-old problem: "Where the hell are they?" It increases the chances that clues will be found, sign will be seen, and tracks will be acted upon. Don't we have an obligation to do all we can when we claim to know what we are doing? After all, we said we would look for their "baby," and that implies that we know how and will be successful.

> **Tracking offers another tool to apply to an age-old problem: "Where the hell are they?"**

Consider these thoughts when you are confronted with situations that cause you to hurry, improvise or "punt:"

1. Only a tracker can determine whether or not tracking can be effective in any given situation. A jump-tracking Incident Commander is not a tracker.

2. Only trackers can decide when, how, and how thoroughly to search for subtle sign and track. Do not be pushed into hurrying. It does not work. Don't be stampeded into making mistakes.

3. Do not believe that tracking will always work. Nothing always works.

4. Tracking is most effective when applied within an effective management scheme. Organization and leadership are always important.

5. Always be track aware. Be aware that for every mile that a person walks, there are thousands of clues. Find them!

6. Do not concentrate on determining if and when tracking will NOT work. Rather, concentrate on how tracking can work every time. Make it happen. Think that it will work. Occasionally, you may be wrong.

7. Deal only with the facts. When inundated with theories, write down the facts and use them to develop a theory rather than searching for facts to substantiate one.

8. Work hard and NEVER give up. Someone is depending on you.

> I have been told on two occasions by search commanders, and one time in front of a reporter, "We didn't call trackers because they always find them and trackers get all the credit. Our searchers need credit too!" This kind of stupidity does exist and, I guess, could only be controlled by retroactive birth control. However, because of education brought on through search management courses, I have seen a substantial decrease in the number of ego-driven search commanders.
>
> – Ab Taylor

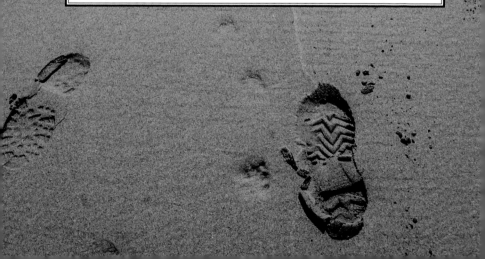

After Benjamin Franklin had received a letter thanking him for having done a kindness, he replied:

As to the kindness you mention, I wish I could have been of more service to you than I have been, but if I had, the only thanks that I should desire are that you would always be ready to serve any other person that may need your assistance, and so let good offices go around, for mankind are all of a family. As for my own part, when I am employed in serving others I do not look upon myself as conferring favors but paying debts.

APPENDICES

Missing Person Questionnaire

Incident Name:_____

Initial Data Capture: _____   Date/Time: _____

Updated By: _____   Date/Time:_____

Updated By: _____   Date/Time:_____

Updated By: _____   Date/Time:_____

Updated By: _____   Date/Time:_____

Sections

First Notice

Please fill all boxes, answer all questions, and print clearly without the use of unfamiliar abbreviations and/or confusing phrases/words. (First Notice information = sections A–E only.)

General and Informant Information A

Case Name/Number:	Agency/Org:
Date: Time:	Location:
Interviewer Name:	Title: Agency/Org:
Reported missing by:	DOB:
Address:	
Home Phone:	Bus. Phone:
Mobile Phone:	Other Phone(s):
Occupation:	Employer:
Email(s):	
Relationship to subject:	
Where can be reached in next 24 hours:	
What does this person think happened?	
Where does this person think the subject is?	
Search efforts prior to calling for SAR:	
Instructions to informant:	
Other persons interviewed (name, contact info, date, time, relationship, DOB):	

Missing Person B

Full Name:	Nickname(s):
Name to call:	Alias(es):
Safe word? Y N Word:	Who knows it:
Subject's primary language:	Speaks English? Y N
Other languages spoken:	Sign Language? Y N

Home address:	
Home Phone:	Bus. Phone:
Mobile Phone:	Other Phone(s):
Occupation:	Employer:
Email(s):	
Category(ies) of lost subject:	
General experience and familiarity with area:	
General quality/quantity of equip. carried and preparedness for environment:	
Police Record:	
Comments:	

Physical Description   C

Age:	Race:	Gender:	Hgt:	Wt:	DOB:

Build:					

Hair Color:	Length:	Style:

If balding, describe:	Eye Color:

Describe all facial hair:			

Glasses	Regular:	Sun:	Contacts:

Describe glasses:

Eyesight without glasses:

Facial features, shape:

Complexion:

Distinguishing marks, scars, tattoos:

Fingerprints on file?	Y	N	Where?	Fake nails?	Y	N

General appearance:

Clothing Worn When Last Seen   D

Hat/Cap/Scarf:

Shirt/Blouse:

Trousers:

Dress:

Sweater/Pullover:

Coat/Jacket/Rain Gear:

Footwear:

Sole pattern and how known:

Hose/Socks:

Underwear:

Other:

Describe all accessories worn such as belt, rings, watch, pins, necktie, tie clip, etc.

Details of Incident   E

Location missing from:

Point last seen (PLS):

Last known point (LKP):

Day/Date last seen:	Time last seen:

Last seen by whom:

Accompanied by animal(s)? (describe):

Vehicle description, if driving:

Destination(s), stated intentions:

Possible alternative destinations:

Route, possible route, how determined:

Weather at time of loss:

Use computer software to determine route(s)?		What used?
Access to this computer?	Where?	

Other resources used to plan trip/outing (books, guides, maps, brochures):

Events of last 24 hours leading up to time of loss:

Familiar with area?

Person most familiar with area? Hazards? Contact info:

Equipment Carried   F

Describe ALL items carried such as pocketbook, wallet, backpack (describe contents of each), matches, lighter, keys, pocket knife, camera, weapon, ammunition, etc. (style, color, brand, size). Use additional pages, if necessary.

Describe any food and water and/or drinks carried, including alcohol:

Describe any pets or animals:
(circle pets thought to be with subject now)

Electronic Device				Battery			
Carried?	Y	Type	Status	Spare?	Type	Last Changed	
Cell Phone							
GPS							
Radio							
Beacon							
Location Service							
RF Tracking Device (Project Lifesaver)							

Other:

Mobile Phone	Provider:	Number:	PIN/Password:
	Model: Smart Phone ☐	Attempt to call?	Left message?
	Text message sent?	User know how to text?	Message sent:

GPS	Default settings:	Datum:	Able to set waypoints?
	Able to record routes?	Able to download routes?	Able to go to waypoint?
	Is the computer to which routes were downloaded available?		

Radio frequency:	Radio PL/CG (used?)	Check-in time/interval:
Beacon number:	Beacon registered?	Web password:
RF Track Freq:	RFID #	On Subject:

Other:

Subject's Experience   G

City/Township/County/ State/Country of residence:	How long?
Previous residence:	How long?

Birthplace:

Has the person been the subject of a search before?

If so, describe the details (date(s), circumstances, how long missing, where and when found, condition when found, actions taken by subject, lost in group? (contact info for others in group, etc.)

Additional info and comments:

Physical Health of Subject   H

General physical condition:

Disabilities:

Known medical conditions:

Recent injuries/trauma:	Last meal:

Recent complaints (including minor):

Pregnant?	How long?	Menstruating?

Physician:	Phone:

Address:

Vision   I

Glasses?	Contacts?	Type of Contacts:	Time stay in:

Spare glasses/contacts:	Corrected vision:	Uncorrected vision:

Color blindness?	Type:	Night vision problems?

Other visual problems:	Vision last checked:

Optometrist/Opthalm. contact info:

Mental/Emotional Health   J

General mental health:

Known mental problems:

Suicidal?	Previous attempts (explain):

Is subject dangerous to self or others? (explain)

Does subject have access to, or possibly carrying, a weapon? (if so, describe type and size)	
Are all weapons accounted for?	Ammo accounted for?
Fears and phobias:	
Knowledgeable person:	Contact info:
Title:	Address:
Physician specialist:	Contact info:
Case manager:	Contact info:
Therapist(s):	Contact info:

Medications: Prescription and Non-prescription   K

Med name, strength, dosage, etc.	Affect if not taken	Lethal dose

Identification   L

Driver's License:	No:	Issue Date:
Passport Country:	No:	Issue Date:

Other ID:

Enrolled in MedicAlert®, Safe Return®, or similar program? (describe)

Electronic tracking device? (describe)

Finances M

Credit & ATM cards: List card names and account numbers.

Current and savings accounts: List banks and account numbers.

Does subject have credit cards or check book in possession?	Y	N	Cash Carried:

Describe:

Detailed Subject History N

Single >		Married >		Divorced >		Widowed >		Adopted >	

Spouse's name:	Phone:

Address:

Siblings (name, age, residence – add page if necessary):

Father's name:	Biological Father?	Y	N	Living?	Y	N

Contact info:

Occupation and employer:

Mother's name:	Biological Mother?	Y	N	Living?	Y	N

Contact info:

Occupation and employer:

Other relatives / caregivers who may have info:

Occupation & Employer   O

Primary occupation:		Retired?	Y	N

Employer:	How long?

Contact person:

Previous/Secondary employment:

Education level (describe):

Military service branch:	Reserves?	Y	N	Currently active?	Y	N
Contact person:	Dates of service:					

Religion/belief system:			Active?	Y	N
Contact person:					

Any recent contacts, changes in behavior?

Other persons who may provide info:

Hobbies, Special Interests   P

Experience in outdoors, backcountry:

Survival training/experience:

First aid training/experience:

Favorite places to visit:

Athletic ability, mobility:

Swimmer, ability/non-swimmer:

Active/outgoing or quiet/withdrawn?

Attitude toward authority:

Use of social media:	Facebook?	Y	N	Twitter?	Y	N	Other:

Online nicknames/tags:

Facebook/Twitter Friends/Followers:

Personal   Q

Recent, current or anticipated financial, legal or other problems:

In whom does the subject confide and/or frequently talk to on the phone?

Who last talked to the subject at length?

When and what was the topic?

Does the subject like animals?

Reaction to dogs, horses?

Recent letter or writings (blogs, email, tweets, etc.)?

Does the subject keep a diary/journal/bible/blog?

Does the subject have access to a computer?

   Describe location, user name(s), password(s)

   Has Internet browser been checked?

   Sites of interest?

MySpace / Facebook: Screen name/Aliases

Does subject smoke, drink, use illegal drugs, or abuse legal drugs? (describe in details)

Additional Information and Comments   R

Search Urgency

Remember the lower the number the more urgent the response!!!

A. SUBJECT PROFILE .... _____

Age
Very Young 1
Very Old 1
Other 2-3

Medical Condition
Known or suspected injury or illness 1-2
Healthy 3
Known fatality 3

Number of Subjects
One alone 1
More than one (unless separation suspected) 2-3

B. WEATHER PROFILE .... _____

Existing hazardous weather 1
Predicted hazardous weather (8 hours or less) 1-2
Predicted hazardous weather (more than 8 hours) 2
No hazardous weather predicted 3

C. EQUIPMENT PROFILE .... _____

Inadequate for environment 1
Questionable for environment 1-2
Adequate for environment 3

D. SUBJECT EXPERIENCE PROFILE .... _____

Not experienced, not familiar with the area 1
Not experienced, knows the area 1-2
Experienced, not familiar with the area 2
Experienced, knows the area 3

E. TERRAIN & HAZARDS PROFILE .... _____

Known hazardous terrain or other hazards 1
Few or no hazards 2-3

TOTAL .... _____

If any of the seven categories above are rated as a one (1), regardless of the total, the search could require an emergency response.

••• THE TOTAL SHOULD RANGE FROM **7** TO **21** WITH **7** BEING THE MOST URGENT. •••

8-11 Emergency Response   *12-16 Measured Response*   *17-21 Evaluate & Investigate*

Track Identification Form

Location of Print:_____

SKETCH:

Date:_____ Time:_____ Heading:_____

Which measurement are you using for sketch? **INCHES** (Imperial) **CM** (Metric)

Sole Type:_____ Overall Pattern:_____

Ground Description:_____

Approx. Age of Print:_____

Stride:_____ Straddle:_____

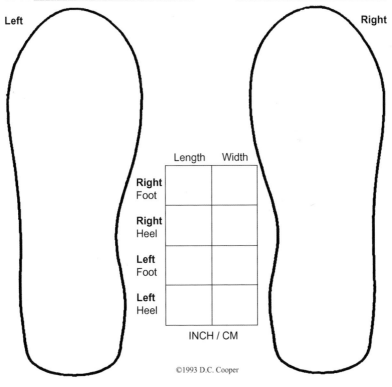

Left

Right

	Length	Width
Right Foot		
Right Heel		
Left Foot		
Left Heel		

INCH / CM

©1993 D.C. Cooper

Track Identification Form

Date:_____ Time:_____ Location:_____

Mission Name:_____ Mission #:_____

Tracker:_____ Op. Period:_____

SUBJECT
Name:_____ Age:_____

Address:_____

Height:_____ Weight:_____ Sex: M F

Physical Problems:_____

Physical Condition:_____

Footwear Sample Available?
YES   NO

FOOTWEAR
Type:_____ Description:_____
Overall   *Heel*
Length:_____ Width:_____ Length:_____ Width:_____

DISCARDABLES
Outer Wear:_____

Shirt:_____ Pants:_____

Inner Wear:_____

Head Wear:_____ Rain Wear:_____

Smoke:_____ Candy/Gum:_____

Other:_____

_____

_____

_____

_____

GLOSSARY

Ab Taylor - old, gnarly, bow-legged rascal that could drink beer nearly as well as he could tell a story—both of which he liked to do simultaneously whenever possible. Also, a man who inspired generations with unparalleled dedication to his craft, his family, and the vulnerable.

Aging sign and track - the ability to determine how long ago a particular piece of sign or track was produced.

Anterior - a medical term used to refer to something toward the front of the body or toward the head.

Arch - the bottom, medial part of the foot just forward of the ankle that curves above the ground. It stretches from the calcaneus to the three medial metatarsals and is sometimes referred to as the "medial longitudinal arch."

Biological forces - energy applied through the nature of living matter.

Bracketing - an occasionally acceptable method of interpolation that uses a predetermined stride to skip one step in sequence in order to find the next, and then use it to find the one skipped.

Brief or **briefing** - exchange of information, usually at the onset of a situation, that conveys important knowledge from the upper levels of a hierarchy to the lower. i.e., information from the Incident Commander conveyed to a tracking team before they begin their assignment.

Chronological order or **chronology** - the arrangement of events in order of occurrence.

Clue conscious or **clue consciousness** - aware that clues exist.

Complete print - the entire impression is visible.

Conclusively Human sign - evidence (sign) which, on its own, can be said to have been definitely caused by a person and not an animal.

Corroborant sign - disturbance that is not decisively human and could have been caused by an animal. It cannot be determined to have been definitely caused by a person, but may confirm or substantiate other evidence with which it may be found.

Crease - sign, usually on soft leaves, that resembles a straight fold in paper.

Cuttable area - a reasonably good area for cutting sign.

Debrief or **debriefing** - exchange of information, usually at the close of a situation, that conveys important knowledge and experience from the lower levels of a hierarchy to the upper; i.e., information conveyed to the Incident Commander from a tracking team after completing an assignment.

Evader - one who avoids and/or resists being followed or found.

Evidence - something legally acceptable before a court, such as an object or a witness, which bears on or establishes an issue. In tracking, evidence is divided into physical and incorporeal.

Excrement - waste matter, usually of human origin. Also, that which flows from the lips of theorists.

Fact - a thing which happened or is real.

Feces - see "excrement."

Flanker - member of a three-person tracking team standing on either side of the Point and who helps discover sign, usually from a standing position.

Forefoot - the larger part of the foot forward of the ankle.

Gait - the pattern of how a person walks.

Steppage gait is when one walks with a foot drop where the foot hangs with the toes pointing down, causing the toes to scrape the ground while walking and requiring the walker to lift the leg higher than normal when walking.

Waddling gait is a duck-like walk where the lateral distance between footfalls can be larger than a normal gait.

Game trail - common route of travel for animals, large and small, that usually follows the path of least resistance in terms of terrain and vegetation.

Heel - the back part of the foot below the ankle.

Identifiable print - a complete or partial print that has at least one characteristic which differentiates it from others similar to it.

Incident Commander - individual charged with functional responsibility for entire incident. Not necessarily highest ranking official, just the one in charge.

Incorporeal evidence - intangible, non-physical information or knowledge which is legally acceptable before a court and which bears on or establishes an issue.

Intoeing - see "pigeon toed."

Jump tracking - an unskilled form of tracking that involves finding an obvious footprint, then proceeding along the presumed direction of travel until another obvious track is found.

Labeling tracks or prints - the action of marking prints so that right, left, and identifiability is indicated.

Lateral - a medical term used to describe something situated away from the middle or to the side of the body; usually to the left or the right.

Lost (or missing) person profile - a vivid biographical and character sketch of a lost person derived from information gleaned through investigation, interviewing, and the Lost (or Missing) Person Questionnaire.

Lost (or Missing) Person Questionnaire - a written document that describes every available physical and mental characteristic of a lost or missing subject.

Lost subject - person being tracked in a search and rescue situation.

Mechanical - of, in accordance with, or using the principles of the science of mechanics. Usually involves the motion of objects or the action of forces on objects.

Medial - a medical term that describes something that is situated toward the middle or midline of the body.

Partial print - only part of the impression is visible.

Perimeter cutting - sign cutting around the boundary or outer edge of an area.

Phalanges - the bones of the toes (and fingers).

Physical evidence - object(s) legally acceptable before a court which bear on or establish an issue.

Pigeon toed - when one walks with the toes pointed medially. This is sometimes called "intoeing" and the medical terms *metatarsus varus* or *metatarsus adductus* may also be used.

Point - member of a three-person tracking team that leads the act of sign discovery, usually from a position just ahead of, and between, the Flankers.

Posterior - a medical term used to describe something toward the back of the body.

Print - an impression left from the passage of a person that can be positively identified as being human.

Pronation (of the foot) - rotation of the medial bones in the midtarsal region of the foot inward and downward so that in walking the foot tends to come down on its inner margin.

Quarry - anything being pursued.

Resource - any thing, person, action, etc. to which one turns for aid in time of need. Something that lies ready for use.

SAR - abbreviation for Search and Rescue.

Scat - waste matter, usually of non-human origin.

Shine - any nearly imperceptible compression of soil or vegetation which reflects light shined from a very oblique angle such that, unlike any other type of sign, it is easier to see from a distance than close up.

Sign - any evidence of change from the natural state that is inflicted on an environment by a person's or an animal's passage.

Sign cutting or **cutting sign** - looking for sign in order to establish a starting point from which to track. Usually performed perpendicular to the direction of travel of a subject.

Sign cutting stick or **tracking stick** - a walking stick-type device used by trackers to measure stride. Furthermore, it assists in focusing attention where the tracker should be looking for sign and not everywhere else.

Splayed feet - when the toes point outward (laterally) when walking; the opposite of intoeing. Sometimes referred to as "toe out."

Step-by-Step Method - a disciplined system for teaching tracking where a tracker sees each step in sequence and proceeds no further than the last visible track, using stride to determine where next to look for sign.

Straddle - the lateral distance between footfalls, perpendicular to the direction of travel.

Supination (of the foot) - a movement of the foot and leg in which the foot rolls outward with an elevated arch so that in walking the foot tends to come down on its outer edge.

Tarsals - the big bones of the foot below and including the ankle and the calcaneus.

Theory - a speculative idea or plan as to how something might be done. Can also be applied to an attempt to explain the unknown.

Toe out - see "splayed feet."

Track - an impression left from the passage of a person or an animal.

Track aware - conscious that sign, tracks, and prints exist and may be useful.

Tracking - following someone or something by stringing together a continuous chain of their sign. Following a chronology of sign.

Track trap - an area particularly good for detecting sign i.e., sand, mud, snow, etc. May be man-made by clearing off an area so that sign would be more easily detected if a subject subsequently passed through.

Tracking team - a three-person group, comprised of a Point and two Flankers, and organized specifically to track.

Urgency - the need for action. For tracking, it is based on quantifiable criteria set forth on an Urgency Determination Form.

INDEX

NOTES